Heinsohn, don't you ever smile?

Heinsohn, don't you ever smile?

THE LIFE & TIMES OF TOMMY HEINSOHN & THE BOSTON CELTICS

By Tommy Heinsohn
with Leonard Lewin

1976
DOUBLEDAY & COMPANY, INC.
GARDEN CITY, NEW YORK

All Photographs From The Collection of Tommy Heinsohn.

ISBN 0-385-11336-6
LIBRARY OF CONGRESS CATALOG CARD NUMBER 75–29885

To my family and friends who made this possible.
TH

Heinsohn, don't you ever smile?

1

HEY, YOU," snarled Wilt Chamberlain. "If you get in my way one more time, I'm gonna kill you."

"Oh, yeah, big baby," I replied in my bravest tone. "Give it a go whenever you're ready."

Damn that Red Auerbach. Always getting me in trouble. Now he had Chamberlain, the world's strongest man, threatening to tear me apart. Why did it always have to be me when it came time for Red to choose a whipping boy?

Wilt and I weren't exactly the best of friends from the last picture. We had come close two or three times the season of 1959–60, and it was only his first year in the NBA. I already had established somewhat of an image as a fighter in my pro basketball career, which began in 1956, but Chamberlain was not what I had in mind to further that reputation.

There was no avoiding contact with him in those days. In Chamberlain's rookie year, everyone was in awe of him. He was some physical specimen. King Kong in sneakers. Seven foot-two, -three, or whatever. He was bigger than he claimed, which was seven-one. He certainly looked much bigger to me.

He was a powerful man. A tremendous offensive player. His biggest weakness was he couldn't shoot fouls. Everyone in the league played percentages. If he got the ball in low, and you let him wheel into the basket, he had two points.

What we did on the Celtics was to force the man with the ball down the sidelines and pressure him. Bill Russell would sneak out and place himself in front of Wilt so they would have to lob the ball. That would give one of us a chance to steal the pass or, as he was catching it, foul him.

Everyone in the league did that to Wilt. It ran through all the forwards. Of course, you used up all the fouls, but it was the strategy. Wilt was a mild-mannered individual. He was no angry man. He was strong, he no doubt was concerned that, if he hit someone, he would hurt him.

It was miraculous the way he controlled himself in view of the punishment he took. He could have ruined the strategy if he had been capable of making his foul shots. There would be no reason to yank his arms or punch the ball or sometimes tackle him to keep him from powering to the basket for easy points.

I was the lucky Celtic grabbing him most times, and sometimes I wondered if he might just lift me up with the ball and jam both through the hoop. He got to know Tommy Heinsohn very well under the circumstances, and I suspected it was a matter of time until he lost his patience.

It finally happened one night in Philadelphia during a regular-season game. A fight started and for some illogical reason Wilt went after me. I had no idea of what I intended to do or what he intended to do to me, but my life flashed before me. Why did Auerbach have to ask me to do his dirty work against someone so big? Why couldn't I give a foul to little Guy Rodgers or to Normie Drucker, a small referee?

Anyway, there I was, waiting for last rites as Wilt came at me. He grabbed me in front of the Philadelphia bench and dug his fingers into my reinforced shoulder straps and ripped out a handful of uniform. That's like tearing the Manhattan phone book apart. You've got to be strong to do that.

Right there and then I made up my mind I'm never going to get too involved with Mr. Chamberlain. I would do what I was told to do because no one should ever accuse me of being a coward, but I would be cautiously brave where Wilt was concerned. This man was capable of dribbling me.

The season progressed and there was another occasion when we were under the boards and bouncing off each other—me more than he, naturally. He looked at me and I stared at him. He looked down, of course, and I looked up. We glared at each other so long I got a stiff neck, but nothing really happened. I got his message, though. He was telling me he was tired of my being a nuisance. It would behoove me to go to the record book and look up the statistics: Wilt Chamberlain, 7-1 (and more), 250 pounds; Tommy Heinsohn, 6-7, 218.

I understood what Wilt had in mind, but I also understood what Auerbach had in mind. Red wanted Chamberlain sent to the foul line instead of scoring baskets and, despite the lurking danger (to me), Auerbach kept urging me to attack at no risk to him.

It's like the kid in the candy store who reached up to touch the candy and got rapped by the owner. "Go on, kid," said a tough-looking truck driver watching the scene. "Touch the candy." Encouraged, the kid reached up and touched the candy, again. He got rapped, again.

Now the truck driver, towering over the meek-looking store owner, looked at the kid and snarled: "Go on, kid. *You* touch *that* candy." The kid, slightly hesitant but reassured by the tone of the truck driver's voice, reached up and touched the candy and got rapped, again.

He looked at the truck driver for support—for something. "Hey, kid," said the driver. "You better not touch that candy because the owner is going to knock your brains out." That's how I felt about my assignment. Auerbach kept urging me to make contact with Wilt and I was in danger of having my brains knocked out.

It built up all season. I could see it in Wilt's eyes. He exploded in the playoffs because of a favorite play we employed to exploit Wilt's slowness making the transition from offense to defense. He was not the fastest person in the world though he ran the quarter mile in high school and could cover ground once his long legs got moving. We would whip the ball into Bob Cousy after a foul shot, and Bill Russell would take off for two easy points. Wilt just couldn't get up the floor with Russ, especially if Bill had a quick start.

Wilt was not dumb. Besides his obvious physical qualities, he had a sharp basketball mind. He began to catch on to the play. We would beat Philadelphia by ten or twelve points and get nine or ten points on this play alone. When we reached the playoffs, Auerbach decided we had to do something else to Wilt.

We were in the fourth year of our dynasty. We won the first championship in Celtic history in 1957—the rookie season for me and Russell—then lost to the St. Louis Hawks in 1958 and beat the Minneapolis Lakers in 1959. Philadelphia and Chamberlain were to be the opening opponents in our 1960 title defense, so Auerbach called a strategy meeting.

"Anytime a foul shot is taken," he told us, "the man who is taking the foul shooter is going to step in and pick off Chamberlain so Russ can take off." Fine. Good strategy. Wilt will turn to head upcourt and a Celtic will impede his progress. But which Celtic?

Red didn't tell us right away. He waited for someone to volunteer. Who in his right mind would sacrifice himself to get in Wilt's way? That's like asking someone to step in front of a subway train to slow it down so a friend can get off. There were no volunteers.

Who got the job for a change? Why, old whipping boy. "Heinsohn," said Red, "you will do this." I looked at him. "We're going to play seven games," I said, assuming the series would go seven, "and I've got to do this against this guy? What's the matter with you?"

Frank Ramsey didn't want to do it because he was too small. Jim Loscutoff, our muscleman, wasn't playing enough at that late stage of his career to be on the floor to do it. I was the logical lamb. On every Philadelphia foul shot, I blocked the shooter and then jumped in Wilt's way.

After Wilt took a few steps, he had a good head of steam going. I got in his way and he ran into me. There were awesome collisions throughout the first game, which we won in the Boston Garden, 111–105. Wilt got forty-two points and twenty-nine rebounds in his first playoff game, an exceptional performance for a rookie.

We knew Wilt was unhappy. I knew because I felt the heat from the big dragon everytime I embarrassed him by picking him off so Russ could break away on foul shots. Russ knew because he blocked at least half a dozen of Wilt's shots. What we didn't know was what, if anything, Wilt would do about it in the second game, which was played on his court in Philadelphia.

Auerbach made sure to remind me of my special assignment,

and Wilt quickly reminded me I would be a lot safer taking my wife to a movie. He advised me what would happen if I got in his way once more. It was a choice between Auerbach and Chamberlain, and for some stupid reason Red won.

I kept bumping Wilt, and each time he hit me harder. In a situation like that, you get cute. I figured Wilt would continue to retaliate so why not alert the referee and get a foul called on Chamberlain? I turned to Arnie Heft, one of the officials, and told him to watch Wilt because he was pushing me all night. I assumed Wilt would get caught on the second action any my picking him off would be tolerated under the rules.

I picked him off at the foul line and he finally hit me a shot from behind so hard, I ended up at halfcourt. He ran up to finish me off. Here comes this seven-one monster pounding up the floor at me: glomp, glomp. He wound up to throw a punch just as I was scrambling off the floor to defend myself. I was about halfway up when Tommy Gola ran between us as a peacemaker just as Wilt let one go, hitting Gola in back of the head. Wilt cracked his hand and was standing there in obvious pain, helplessly.

With great courage and glee, I assumed my best James J. Corbett fighting stance and pelted the giant with lefts and rights but he didn't even know I was hitting him. There was a picture in the paper the next day that showed Wilt down and me standing over him. I didn't know how he hit the floor. It certainly wasn't from any of my punches. That's probably where Muhammad Ali got the idea for that part of his act where he fakes being knocked down.

They took Wilt to the hospital and taped his hand so he could play the third game, in Boston. It was his right hand—the shooting hand—and it was heavily bandaged, but to his credit he insisted on playing.

Auerbach was equally insistent we follow the same strategy. That meant little old me picking off big old Wilt on foul shots again. Red figured Wilt had another hand, so go get him, baby. Sometime in the third game, they lobbed the ball over Russell's head and I couldn't possibly get to Wilt before he went into the act of shooting. The pressure was on me.

There was only one thing to do. I swung at the ball, hoping to punch it from his hands. He was so strong, there really was no way you could take the ball away from him. I ended up punching him on his bandaged hand. He went through a series of weird steps that reminds me of today's dances.

They charged me with a foul, and Wilt glared as he walked to the line in pain. I said to myself: "Oh, no. If this guy comes after me again, what am I going to do now?" I stared at him and he stared at me. And that was the last time Wilt Chamberlain and I had any kind of problem. He thought I was nuts. He probably said: "This guy's crazy. He broke my hand and then goes and punches me on the broken hand. I better leave him alone."

It's strange how something that happened when I was in the first or second grade probably prepared me for Wilt Chamberlain and other confrontations in life. I guess Celtics are made, not born. The lesson I learned at six or seven established the confidence and boldness that characterizes the winning attitude of Celtics as individuals and as a team.

We lived in Jersey City at the time. My father worked for the National Biscuit Company in Newark. My mother worked for Woolworth's in town. I had one sister, Marion, 4½ years younger. I had an extremely difficult time as a youngster mainly because our neighborhood was predominately Irish and Italian. I happened to be the only German within hitting distance and it was World War II, so I was the bad guy.

There were two Italian families—the DePintos and Perullis—and a clan of Irishmen named O'Brien. There were a lot of kids in all the families. Relatives and cousins lived with them. They probably all had gone to see the war movies together. You know, John Wayne and *Back from Bataan* and the Nazi films about Hitler and General Rommel.

I was the only German they could get their hands on, so every day the three families would line up and Heinie had to run for home. There were at least twelve of them all the time to one of me. Every day the same old way and it got to the point where I wouldn't go out of the house after school.

I tried getting cute, even at that age. I told the Italian kids I didn't know why they were acting that way because I was German and they should be on my side. It didn't work. They kicked the hell out of me, anyway.

I just couldn't go out and play anymore. I began hanging around the house and my mother got upset. She knew what was going on but she couldn't force me to take another beating. I would rather take one from her. For some reason, it didn't hurt as much. Finally she convinced my father he had to do something about it. She didn't want her little boy Tommy acting like a shut-in. It wasn't healthy. As far as I was concerned, it was a lot healthier than trying to escape the DePintos, Perullis, and O'Briens.

My father decided to take a day off from work to resolve the situation. "All right, Tommy," he said. "You're going out and you're going to see those guys." I had no choice. We went out and my father rounded up a half dozen of assorted DePintos, Perullis, and O'Briens.

We had this small enclosure at the side of our house. I remember my father telling the kids that I was going to fight them. There were no objections. Why not? They had the greatest record for boxing until Rocky Marciano retired unbeaten.

"Which one," my father said to me, "would you like to fight?" I looked them over. I was smart even in those days, so I chose the smallest kid. "Not him," said my father, who must have studied under Red Auerbach. "Let's take him." He picked the biggest kid, naturally.

All my father told me was to do whatever the other kid did to me. If he kicked, I should kick. If he bit, I should bite. I had about two years of humiliation and anger inside me and I was all over that kid, much to his and my surprise.

I think I fought all six kids that day. I had never pushed myself to stand up to anyone before, but this time I did. The mere fact that my father brought them one at a time into the enclosure and assured a fair fight gave me the courage. I don't remember the scorecard. I think I won a few and lost a few.

There were fringe benefits from that living experience. During the time when I was afraid to leave the house, I began making model planes and started to draw. It was before we had television, so I learned to survive by myself. I guess my parents do not realize to this day that my interest in painting originated at that time.

I think the entire experience provided me with the discipline that is necessary to drive yourself for something you want. I learned to do things by and for myself and gained a determination not to let anyone push me around. I remember what my father told me when I was through fighting the kids: "Don't start anything, but finish what you start."

It's funny how things work out. I had a similar experience with my son Paul, who is developing into quite an athlete. He is the sports nut. My other son, David, is the artist. He loves to paint and play the piano. He obviously gets his sensitivity and compassion from his father, as any NBA referee will tell you. My daughter Donna Marie, the oldest, was a dancer and cheerleader and in one respect was lucky she didn't take after her mother, since Diane was a basketball player in her time.

That's another story for another time. Let me tell you about Paul and the time he became interested in the Pop Warner Football League. He was nine years old and was having the same type of problem I had in the neighborhood when I was a kid, except his was more social. He was tall for his age and everyone thought he was at least eleven.

He became kind of isolated because of that. He was a rough, tough kid, and the mothers in the neighborhood were afraid to allow their children to play with him. When he play-wrestled it was like Victor the Bear, who used to wrestle fans invited out of the stands at NBA games.

One day Johnny Most, the announcer for the Celtic games, suggested the Pop Warner League as a release for Paul's young energy. Paul went to practice for about three or four weeks, and then the day before the first ball game he said he was going to quit. I was puzzled. He seemed to like it. It was organized. There were kids there and he was accepted.

I was happy to see him involved with sports because to a large degree they are a way of acceptance. Efforts are appreciated and a young man can make his mark and establish a degree of identity. Paul didn't understand all the values and refinements but he was enjoying himself and he was occupied, which was what Diane and I were mostly concerned about.

It was like when I first discovered basketball. We didn't have organized leagues at that time. We played two-on-two and three-on-three in the schoolyard. My father's interest was fundamentally in my being involved in something.

He would come to the schoolyard on a Saturday afternoon and sit on the wall as I played. He learned the game while I was learning it. He never pushed me to perfection. He never lived vicariously through my participation in sports. He never placed any undue pres-

sures on me, which is the real danger of organized sports for young
people.

To this day, he comes to the games with my mother when the
Celtics play in New York, and he's always going through the scrap-
books my wife has kept since I was in high school. All he ever said
to me was: "You played a great game" or "You played a lousy
game." I had no intention of doing otherwise with Paul, other than
he had to pay the penalty of having two basketball experts in the
family—his mother and father.

I assumed the Pop Warner thing was fine for him. It was his first
experience with football. He never watched it on television. He never
was involved in it. It was a physical thing and he liked it. They'd
teach him how to block and tackle. How to buckle on his helmet and
all such things.

I would take him to practice when I could, but most of the time
he went with Diane. The Saturday before the first game Paul told me
he was going to quit. I told him that was okay with me if that was
what he wanted, but since he had gone this far, why not at least play
the first game. "Well," he said, "I don't have the shoes. If I don't
have the shoes, I don't want to play."

I convinced him it was better to play a game and decide if he
liked it before we invested in football shoes. He agreed, reluctantly. I
took him to the game the next day and discovered he was on the
kickoff team. I figured like any kickoff team, this was the suicide
squad and he would be making a brief appearance.

Much to my surprise, he also was on the starting defensive team.
He was a tackle. He was a big kid so they put him at a position
where they could use his size. He didn't do too badly for his first
game, and I was impressed. He had joined a team that had not won
in thirty-three games and it went ahead 8–0 in the third quarter.

Naturally, there was a lot of noise and excitement. If you have
ever had a son or daughter involved in the Little League, you can
appreciate the yelling and screaming that went on. The game moved
into the fourth quarter, and the other team put on a sustained drive.
Normally a Pop Warner team fumbles or makes some mistake to
give up the ball, but the other team put it all together for forty yards
—punching it out five, six yards at a time. Nothing really big.

It was like the Boston Patriots against the New York Jets. It became third down and two yards to go from the twelve with time running out. Paul's team had a big, fat coach and he was on the sidelines screaming: "Heinsohn! Heinsohn! Get the quarterback!" Sure enough, they snapped the ball and Paul jumped through the line and got the quarterback for about a six-, or seven-yard loss.

That stopped the drive, and Paul's team wound up winning, 8–0. You would think they had just won the Super Bowl. Everyone went wild. They crowded around Paul and pounded him for making the big play. He was all smiles. He was a hero.

Now we are in the car going home and I asked how he had liked it. "Oh, Dad," he said, "I loved it. It was terrific. Gee, Dad. It was great. What fun."

He was totally enthusiastic. "I guess," I said, "now we'll get you the shoes." I told him how impressed I was over his starting and that he had played so well. "In fact," I said, "you made the key play. It was third down and two to go, you busted through the line and nailed the quarterback and that really stopped their drive. I thought that was terrific. You won the game."

He looked at me. He obviously was deeply moved by the praise coming from his father. "Dad," he said, "I'd like to ask a question." I nodded. "Sure, what is it?" I replied, wondering what could puzzle him at that exciting moment in his life. "What's third down, Dad?" he asked innocently.

I'm sure Paul's first football shoes meant as much to him as my first basketball had meant to me. I was eleven at the time and the family had moved to Union City—away from the DePintos, Perullis, and O'Briens. There were no fights in that neighborhood. It was all basketball once I discovered the game.

I would say the only eventful thing that occurred during that stage of my growing up took place where I spent most of my time shooting baskets. It had about a twenty-foot ceiling and was so low that I had to shoot line drives. If you had fired thousands of shots that way, you wouldn't shoot any other way, either. That's how I became a line-drive shooter.

I was just another kid growing up in Union City, New Jersey, with a sort of neighborhood reputation for being on the winning side in schoolyard ball. There was nothing really distinctive in my life until I made the high school basketball team at St. Michael's and received my first important recognition by the news media. My name had appeared in the box scores and occasionally was mentioned in a story, but then came the big one in December of 1950.

We played the Demarest Red Wings and beat them, 44–42. I was high scorer with twenty-three points and made ten baskets. This was the headline: "Irish Uncover Scoring Phenom in 'Whitey' Heinsohn and Win." In the body of the story, it said: "Tom 'Whitey' Heinsohn, a lanky junior who has developed with leaps and bounds, was the key man in Coach Patty Finnegan's alignment, both defensively and offensively. The white-haired one took the evening's scoring honors with twenty-three points and tallied the winning basket in the last ten seconds of play."

Would you believe it? Whitey Heinsohn. How times do change.

2

I WANTED TO play football desperately in high school. Football was a big thing in New Jersey. Besides, there was a young lady named Diane Regenhard I wanted to impress. She was in my homeroom and she was a beauty.

I had made it my top priority to get to know her. One day I was passing out books and deliberately ignored her. I walked by her four or five times and then began making remarks. I finally got up enough courage to ride to her house on my bicycle. We started to go together as high school freshmen and, the day after I was graduated from Holy Cross and before I became a member of the Boston Celtics, I married the girl.

She was a majorette at the football games, so I wanted to play football. I had a wonderful experience with football. I was the first one cut from the team every year. I was 6-1 as a freshman and weighed something like 130 pounds. They never had a pair of pants that fit me, so they dropped me from the team.

There was another consideration. I was so skinny they were afraid they would have to hold up the game too long to pick up the pieces if I got hit. When I got to college, there were people who tried to get me to play football but my career had ended by then. In high school, I established a perfect record that still stands at St. Michael's: most ignored, four years.

I found a way to get into the high school football games for nothing. I became an important cog in the marching band. You know the kid with the drum? That was me. It created problems I never anticipated.

I was playing basketball at the time and, as my reputation grew, all the fellows I knew from other schools would wait for the marching band and taunt the hell out of me. I wanted to quit but they wouldn't let me. I was forced to pay the penalty just because I was the only one in school capable of playing the tenor drum.

I had learned to play because all the kids in my neighborhood in Union City were interested in the Drum and Bugle Corps, a status symbol in those days. I think I was in the sixth grade when I began beating the drums. All the fellows with whom I played ball were in the Corps, so I got involved for the social aspects. It was the thing to do.

Little did I realize I would grow up to the high school marching band and such taunts as: "There he goes, the All-County kid with his white pants. Why can't you get bigger pants?" and "Look at the big drum and the bigger schmuck behind it." I was a lanky kid and my white ducks always were above my ankles.

We had to march from the school up to the football stadium, which was about two miles. And there they were, the guys I played basketball against, lined up along the way and having a great time at my expense. No hotshot basketball player was supposed to be in the band, and they took advantage of the opportunity to let me know.

I tried every which way to quit. In my junior year, they called practice and I didn't show. The next thing I knew, the principal sent for me and told me I'm going to be in the band. A biology teacher we called the Jeep because she buzzed around like a Jeep also put on the pressure.

This nun really liked me. She was taking her masters in biology at Fordham and I helped her with the homework. She would send me up to the top room, like in the attic, to do the drawings for her.

By then I was pretty good as an artist, so I would draw the plates—you know, what an amoeba and paramecium looked like. I did all the drawing homework. In effect, I passed the course for her.

She just happened to be head of the band as well as my homeroom teacher. A homeroom teacher had such weapons as making you stay after school and other ways of making one's life miserable. I waited until my junior year when she no longer was my homeroom teacher to quit, and it lasted just one day.

In she marched with the principal into one of my classrooms, and they escorted me outside. They informed me I was the only tenor drummer in school and, if I was going to be obstinate, they wanted to see my parents to discuss it. So I ended up as the top drummer of the marching band at St. Michael's for five or six football games a year and never regretted it.

Like everything in life, there were advantages and disadvantages. The disadvantage was the ridicule. The advantages were I got into the football games for nothing and was close to my girlfriend, the majorette. I never developed into a Gene Krupa, but he can't shoot a basketball, either.

By putting a basketball through the hoop so well, I developed an opportunity to go to almost any college of my choice. A strange thing began happening that I did not understand until many years later. I became something special because I had an unusual talent in sports.

I made All-Star teams. I was invited to play in the North-South game involving the best high school players in the country. I was named to the All-America high school team. My name was in the papers all the time. People looked at me in a special way.

Most people don't look at everybody. But I was Tommy Heinsohn, basketball player, so people looked at me and wanted to talk to me. You do not realize it, but there is a pressure that builds inside you that most athletes find difficult to handle once it all ends. I know because it happened to me when I had to make the transition to a normal life after all the years of basketball and excitement with the Boston Celtics.

It is tremendously difficult to be yourself, what you really are, once you are exposed to pressures that start early in life. You are taken out of the mainstream and people treat you differently. That creates a pressure that at times is so damn subtle. The dinners and all the other ceremonies to which young athletes are subjected affect them and the people around them.

My sister, Marion, for example. She was a fighter before my father made one of me. Once when she was around five or six she beat up a boy in our neighborhood. My father stopped her. "What are you doing?" he said to her. "He punched me," she said. "I saw you walk over and punch him—when did he start the fight?" she was asked. "Last week," she replied.

Marion and I were close as we grew up despite the age difference. Her biggest gripe came when she followed me into high school. They'd say to her: "You're Tommy Heinsohn's sister." She would be furious. She didn't want to be Tommy Heinsohn's sister. She wanted to be Marion Heinsohn. She wanted to be judged on her merits.

That's how special I became because I was a somebody who could win basketball games. Mind you, this was in high school. She came home and hated me. She finally told me so years later when she was twenty and getting ready to be married. It had been tough being Tommy Heinsohn's sister.

It wasn't easy being Tommy Heinsohn, either. People began beating my door down because I was a good ballplayer. Letters from senators. Letters from colleges. Telephone calls. I could have gone to any school in the country. I got around 250 offers, which is about what Wilt Chamberlain received when he finished high school—the closest I ever came to him in the record books.

At that time, there was only one game that really meant anything to the college scouts. The North-South game was like a tryout camp. Chuck Taylor, the promoter, brought the top sixteen high school basketball players to Murray, Kentucky, and worked them twice a day for a week. All the college coaches were able to look over the merchandise.

Chuck Taylor paid the players' expenses, gave them a little spending money, and it was a big thing in their lives at that time. It was a trip away from home and the prestige and the honor of playing the game. They would take you to Kentucky Lake and you would go to fish fries. Can you imagine exciting a Moses Malone with a fish fry? It was not exactly like visiting Marbella, Spain, with the NBA Players' Association and sampling the paiella and the wines, but rather impressive when you are seventeen and it is 1951.

I was one of five players to make the All-Star team from that game, so I could have gone anyplace I wanted. By that time, I already had made up my mind it would be Holy Cross but, in essence, what I'm saying is that the atmosphere was a perfect example of how a basketball player was treated as something special.

I actually started drawing attention from the colleges when I was sixteen. I would hear from someone's brother or cousin or friend. Everybody had a reason why I should go to a certain college. They talked to me and my parents. There were only two people who actually came to my house. One was Dudey Moore of Duquesne and the other Ken Loeffler of LaSalle. I would say that Dudey chased me more than anybody. He went after me through Haskell Cohen, who was the NBA publicity director at the time and also picked an annual All-America high school team for *Parade* magazine.

I remember Haskell sitting next to my father at a game we played in a Catholic high school tournament in Brooklyn. He was scouting me and came to the locker room after the game. I introduced him to my father, and Haskell couldn't believe he was the same man who had sat so quietly in the next seat all night. My father's the same way today.

He sits behind our bench in Madison Square Garden with my mother and you never would know he was there. People say nasty things about his lovable son but he controls himself. If only his son could be like that. My father always believed in offering guidance but being inconspicuous and not overbearing at all times.

He helped me sort out the scholarship offers by asking what I really wanted out of college. I received letters from Notre Dame, the Ivy League. My father, in a rare attempt to influence me, suggested I think about Annapolis. He loved the sea and boats and thought it would be an outstanding program for me.

I ended up going to Holy Cross because it was totally honest with me. Not that the other schools lied about the things they promised if I wore their basketball uniform. By then I was almost six-five and still growing. I could put the ball through the basket more often than most players with line drives or hook shots with either hand, a valuable commodity in the sports market.

I went down to North Carolina State for a weekend. I had try-outs at Niagara. I played against their varsity with my cousin, Eddie Madsen, who later went to St. Bonaventure. I got to know what traveling in the NBA might be like through the trips I made to so many schools. If I had accepted all the invitations, I probably would still be trying out on the campuses.

Some offers made me laugh. For example, they would put my girlfriend through school or anybody else I selected. Money really never was discussed. It always was understood there would be money but I never encouraged anyone, so the discussions never reached that stage.

I decided I wanted to be a doctor and many colleges said I could enter their medical school on scholarship if I played basketball. There were no qualifications until I visited Holy Cross. I went there primarily because of Earle Markey, now a Jesuit priest, who had played freshman ball there when Bob Cousy was a senior.

Togo Palazzi, who also was from Union City, was at Holy Cross at the time. I took the trip to Worcester, Massachusetts, and went to see the people in the administration. I told them I was interested in premed and had sent my grades and all other requirements. I was advised that if I was interested in premed and also playing basketball, Holy Cross was not the place for me. Amazing.

That opened my eyes. All other schools had promised me everything but a shingle alongside Dr. DeBakey's, and Holy Cross told me premed did not mix with basketball. There was no way I could devote the time to medical studies if I was going to play basketball.

I am not one to criticize the system of giving scholarships to athletes. It certainly enabled me to go to college and eventually realize my ambition of playing professional basketball. However, there are extremely dangerous aspects to the wholesale recruiting system. It is uncomfortable for a young man of seventeen or eighteen to be confronted with such pressure. I can appreciate what Wilt Chamberlain experienced before he decided on Kansas University or Moses Malone before he chose Maryland only to accept a million dollars to play for the Utah Stars or Kareem Abdul-Jabbar before he ended his bidding war by enrolling at UCLA.

That can have a terrible effect on the sense of values and minds of people not mature enough to understand such things. My son Paul was only fifteen when he was innocently placed in the middle of a high school recruiting situation. Maybe he was forced to pay the penalty for having the name Heinsohn and, like my sister, Marion, was deeply hurt by what happened.

We live in South Natick, Massachusetts, and the people in the school system were anxious for Paul to go on to the local high school from junior high. He was a fairly good basketball player but a better prospect in football. They wanted him for both sports, but I had decided that I would try and get him into a specific Catholic school outside the district because of academics.

I wanted someone to knuckle him in algebra. I wanted someone looking over his shoulder and disciplining him so he could get the most out of his potential. The Natick school system was capable, but Paul needed more personalized attention. I was willing to pay for that necessity.

I mentioned it to Paul but did not discuss it in depth because he still had to finish junior high. Meanwhile, he was playing CYO ball with some kids from another junior high and they talked one day about going to Marian High so they could be teammates.

Someone coaching one of the CYO teams overheard the conversation about Marian, another Catholic school, and wondered if they had ever thought of Catholic Memorial, which was in the Boston area. It was the second time Paul had heard the name because I had mentioned it to him. I called the CYO coach and learned he was an alumnus of Catholic Memorial but had no other affiliation with the school.

I then called Ron Perry, a former teammate and now athletic director at Holy Cross. He had been a coach and athletic director at Catholic Memorial and gave the high school top recommendations for sports and academics. His son was playing for the school at the time and was an outstanding player.

I was satisfied. My wife drove Paul over to the school to talk to the people and file an application. A story appeared in a Boston newspaper that Paul was going to Catholic Memorial. The name Heinsohn attracted a headline, naturally, whereupon I was informed that, if Paul went there, the school would be brought up on recruiting charges.

They actually tried to frighten my son. He would be suspended and Catholic Memorial would be suspended from all tournament play. In no way, shape, or form was Paul ever recruited unless I was accused of doing it. I explained that to the newspaperman who broke the story, the Natick people, and everyone involved, but it did no good.

You will not believe how a basic interest of a father in his son's welfare mushroomed into a Watergate affair. I called the athletic director at Natick to find out what was going on. "Well," he said, "we have found out your son has been recruited. There have been several visits by an individual to your house to put pressure on the boy."

I was tempted to look under the bed to see if J. Gordon Liddy or Howard Hunt was there. That's how ridiculous it got. I said: "Hey, look. I've been in these sort of things a long time. I assure you personally that there have been no pressures by any school or anyone other than by me, his father. I want him to go to that school."

I repeated the exact story as to how it happened, but he didn't believe me. Then I found out there was an investigation going on and they were to interrogate the CYO coach who had spoken to Paul. The fellow worked for IBM and dug kids and suddenly found himself involved in an inquisition.

I have lost my temper for a lot less in a basketball game. It was too much. Paul was afraid to go to school. My wife was upset. My daughter Donna got some heat because she was a cheerleader at the high school that was making all the trouble. They were trying to trap Paul through her.

I grabbed the phone so hard I almost bent it. I was tired of them questioning Paul, my daughter, and me. I was angry that the Heinsohn family was projected into a local scandal. "Look," I told the athletic director, "if you keep this up, I will have to bring charges against you. You are putting pressure on a fifteen-year-old boy and, if you don't stop, I'll personally write a letter to the Headmasters' Association about this whole matter. Furthermore, I might have to sue you."

What do you think was his reaction? He actually asked if he could bring the coach over to my house to talk to me. Here he was messing up my son's life with charges of recruiting and all he wanted was to have me talk with the coach. For what? To recruit, of course. That was frightening.

Imagine exposing young people to that kind of mentality. No wonder the younger generation is more conscious than we ever were about hypocrisies. It is a sad and serious situation when fifteen-year-old boys are victims of such abuse of power and exploitation.

I really could not blame a local sports columnist for writing: "The real losers in this case are basketball coach Charlie Christie and football coach Bob Whelan. No doubt these gentlemen had big plans for Heinsohn but I am sure, like myself, they are keenly disappointed." That writer apparently did not have a fifteen-year-old son like Paul, the real loser because of the unreasonable and irrational pressure put on him by an athletic director of a high school.

Life is full of traumatic incidents such as that. For example, I remember the first time I walked across the campus at Holy Cross. When I made up my mind to go there, I knew they were going to treat me like a student. That was my motivation for accepting a scholarship to play basketball. I wanted an education, and the only way for me to get it was through basketball.

I had never really been away from home that much. I was eighteen and I walked proudly on the campus for the first time with my powder blue suit and pegged pants. I discovered that was a fine outfit for the streets of Union City but not the thing you wore at Holy Cross. They were all kids with gray flannel suits. Nobody wore pegged pants. And nobody wore powder blue suits.

I strolled casually across the campus with my lone piece of luggage, and all the guys with the charcoal suits stared at me. They were from Larchmont, Boston, and the Newtons. They laughed and said: "Who is this guy?"

That was some start. I ultimately overcame it. I got a gray flannel suit, giving me an extensive wardrobe of two suits. It didn't matter. The only outfit in which I had any interest was a basketball uniform, and it wasn't long before they forgot about the young man without the gray flannel suit.

Our freshman team went unbeaten in fifteen games, and everyone got to know us. I really did not have too much to do with Buster Sheary, the varsity coach, until I was a sophomore, but he liked to have us scrimmage the varsity. He was Mr. Sheary to everybody.

He would come over to the freshmen and say: "Boys, the varsity over there thinks you are a bunch of snot-nosed kids." As I was saying, Celtics are made, not born. He was the Red Auerbach of his time for me. He certainly knew how to motivate a player.

"Even though you are 12–0 right now," Buster said to us, "they think you can't hold their sneakers." That got us going—us being me, Joe Liebler, Don Prohovich, who played in the White Sox chain, Tommy Burke, who became a priest, and Dick Santaniello, who became a teacher in Rhode Island.

Buster, of course, went back to the varsity and advised them of our arrogance. How we thought we were such hotshots because we were unbeaten. I can remember how we played halfcourt and we held the varsity without a basket for twenty minutes. They had Togo Palazzi, Ronnie Perry, Earle Markey, Spike Casey, Dave Nangle, Bob Magilligan from Brooklyn, and Jim Kielley, who was about six-ten.

That made every scrimmage a little Civil War, with General Sheary motivating both sides. He was exceptional at that. He did not waste much time working on me until I became a sophomore and made the starting team because of my freshman exploits and the fact that at six-six I was the tallest on the squad.

I was assigned to play center, and Buster made sure rather quickly I would be prepared for the battle of the big men. I remember we were getting ready for the Sugar Bowl tournament during the Christmas holidays. We were to play DePaul with Ron Sobie, who later played for the Knicks, and the winner undoubtedly would face LSU and Bob Pettit in the final.

This kid Prohovich, who was on the freshman team with me, proceeded to rap me every time I got the ball in scrimmage. He was six-two and he banged me around in the pivot. He pressed me all over the place. I was bigger and his job was to make contact and block me out. He was totally physical to the point where my low boiling point began to heat up.

I suggested he cut it out but he wouldn't stop. It was the German against the neighborhood bullies in Jersey City and I wound up to hit him. All of a sudden Buster Sheary came swooping in. "You big, dumb German," he snarled, "what the hell do you think you're doing?"

I told Mr. Sheary that the man was rapping the hell out of me. He said: "Don't worry about that. I told him to do it. You're gonna get that and more. You better learn to control your temper." I just don't know. Everybody had this thing about my temper.

You think I don't have a thing with my temper? I do get perturbed. Sometimes I even get mad and do something about it. I have had my temper worked on from the moment I was a high school player. People think I have a tremendous temper and I can't control it. That's nonsense. I just express my displeasure but I never lose my rationale, whatever that means.

Mr. Sheary did a wonderful job on my emotions while I was at

Holy Cross. He was the reason why I was never sorry that I had not gone to Notre Dame after having sent my marks there, among a number of other colleges. Notre Dame came back to haunt me the first couple of seasons I played for Holy Cross. But it only hurt for a little while.

Notre Dame was the only team to beat us during the regular season of my sophomore year, which was not a bad one as things turned out. It appeared as though it was all over when the University of Connecticut also beat us out of a berth in the NCAA tournament after Togo Palazzi had put us ahead by three points with eight seconds to go. There was one problem with the basket: The referees ruled that Wally Supronowicz, one of our guards, had stepped out of bounds while flipping the pass back to Togo, so we only led 77–76.

We lost that one, 78–77, but made up for everything by winning the National Invitation Tournament in Madison Square Garden. Our victory over Western Kentucky in the semifinal game was the best example of perfect team execution I ever experienced in all my years of basketball.

Western Kentucky was a run-and-shoot team of all big guys, and Mr. Sheary, a shrewd strategist, had advised us to protect the ball at all times and make sure we took only good-percentage shots. He realized that might take a little patience, so he made sure that Palazzi and Heinsohn, two gunners from the streets of New Jersey, understood the message.

We did until the game started. Togo took the first four shots on the run, and Mr. Sheary called time. "Palazzi," he said in the huddle, "what are you supposed to be doing?" That was straightened out and the game resumed.

Heinsohn took the next five shots on the run and we were eleven points down. Another time-out. "Heinsohn," said Mr. Sheary, his voice a little shriller, "I get Palazzi straightened out and now you go nuts." He finally got it through our thick heads to slow it down and make every move count.

We never made a mistake the rest of the way. We made Mr. Sheary proud of his game plan as we slowed down the Western Kentucky fast break and ran with them when the opportunity was there. Our championship game with Duquesne, the school that had tried so desperately to get me, was not as clinically perfect but we surprised everyone by winning that one, too.

Palazzi was voted the Most Valuable Player but I had some nice things said about me. "Holy Cross was the smartest ballhandling club I've seen all year," said Dudey Moore, the coach of Duquesne. "Those small guys cut off the post very well. But Heinsohn was the guy who beat us. He's better than Stokes all around. Stokes may drive better but Heinsohn works the post better and does more. Heinsohn should have gotten the Most Valuable Player award. He hurt us more than Palazzi." Maurice Stokes was not only one of the finest college players of all time but would have established it in the pros if his career had not been terminated by encephalitis.

I think everyone was wrong. Mr. Sheary should have been named Most Valuable for his coaching job. Duquesne was the second- or third-best team in the country on offense and we just ran them. We used a fast-break, spread offense that is the same one I put in to exploit Dave Cowens' unique talent.

I was the center, and Mr. Sheary used me to pull the center out so we could keep the middle open. That's exactly what we do with Cowens. He opens the middle so we can flash our other people through and make the defense scramble.

Mr. Sheary was responsible for that as he had been responsible for making Holy Cross a national basketball institution. Holy Cross was a small New England school until Bob Cousy, George Kaftan, and Frank Oftring won the NCAA championship in 1948. That made it easier to get ballplayers from the New York and New Jersey areas, the breeding grounds for the thinking man's game.

A lot of me went when Mr. Sheary quit after my junior season. We won the Sugar Bowl and the NIT in my sophomore season, and the next year I was MVP in the Sugar Bowl, though Notre Dame beat us in the championship game. We also went to the NIT final that year and lost to St. Francis of Loretto, Pennsylvania, and the great Maurice Stokes.

Mr. Sheary had been promised a raise by the new head of the college after we had won the NIT. The new president told Mr. Sheary to give him a chance to settle in the job and he would produce more money the next season.

I am sure the president was sincere and had every intention of keeping his word. But he apparently forgot about the commitment when his brother, a prisoner in China for about fifteen years, was released and came home to America. In the confusion and chaos that followed, a contract was sent to Mr. Sheary without the raise, and he returned it with his resignation. He was a proud man of principle.

I felt his loss more than anyone because he had been like a grandfather to me. I didn't enjoy my senior year at all and came close to quitting a few times. I found something distinctively missing after Mr. Sheary had worked on me and everyone emotionally, physically, and strategically for every game.

He was like Knute Rockne. He made you eager to play and prepared you in every way. He and Jackie Whalen, our assistant coach and scout, spent most of the basketball budget on costs for paper for their game plans. By contrast, I heard of one college basketball coach who had his scouting reports for the first two games of the season written on the back of a matchbook cover.

We never were unprepared because of Mr. Sheary and Jackie Whalen, another fine strategist. That didn't mean they always were right. I am sure neither has forgotten the game plan that turned into a Notre Dame victory in my first season. Jackie not only scouted Notre Dame but also solicited an independent survey to substantiate his report that the Irish did not run.

Notre Dame proceeded to fast break our pants off, a most embarrassing development for Mr. Sheary and Mr. Whalen. I learned at an early stage that life was full of embarrassing moments, such as the time I jumped in anger when a high school referee called one the wrong way. I leaped about four feet in the air in a tantrum and, when I descended, my heels skidded and I landed on my can. Some six hundred people laughed, and I joined them. And there are those who think I am the first angry man with no sense of humor.

I never had a fight in high school basketball, though. I think Mr. Sheary was concerned that I would when I was at Holy Cross, which is why he put me through the test quite early with Prohovich. I was already very physical from having played semipro basketball while I was in high school. I played with more mature semi-pros even though I was a skinny kid. I played under assumed names because the high school coach and other officials made it clear you were not supposed to play outside ball. I didn't get paid but I had to use a phony name so they wouldn't discover Heinsohn in the box scores.

I played center for the Woodshed AC team of Union City under the name of Bunnomo and other fictitious names. Every night I had a different name. I always used Irish or Italian names for no specific reason. We played in Jersey City, Newark, and in New York and the constant competition improved my game.

We went across the Hudson River to play the Snookey Sugar Bowl Five at the Harlem YMCA, a tough team that made me tougher. By the time I got to college, anyone who rapped me got rapped back harder. It was all clean but rough fun, and there weren't any fights until I got into the NBA and all those nasty individuals began picking on little old me.

Oh, there were a few skirmishes with the Harlem Globetrotters, but they didn't count. The Globies were famous for their winning streaks, not for fighting. As it turned out, Abe Saperstein would have been better off if the 1956 College All-Star team had boxed the Globies, in view of what we did to their basketball image.

At that point, the Globetrotters were basketball in the minds of many people. They thought the Globies could beat any team in the world. The Globies booked an annual tour against the best college seniors to further that image. They would employ two co-operative referees, and that helped for some strange reason. If they lost, they would change one referee. Saperstein fired him the next day.

We played twenty-one games in nineteen days. Sometimes doubleheaders—one game in the afternoon, one at night. We had Ron Sobie, Joe Holup, Julius McCoy, Si Green, Johnny McCarthy, and a few other outstanding college players. They paid big money. I made about three thousand dollars for the trip. That was better than I was going to make in the NBA under my first contract with the Celtics that called for nine thousand dollars for seventy-two games.

We never practiced, just played. We had an honorary coach in each city. It was so competitive, we had fights almost every night. Woody Sauldsberry and Andy Johnson, both of whom were to play with the Philadelphia Warriors, played and fought for the Globies. Sweetwater Clifton played a little because it was the off-season for the Knicks, who permitted him to pick up a little extra money that way.

Leon Hilliard did the comedy dribbling. Meadowlark Lemon was the clown. We ended up winning eleven of the twenty-one games, with the referees and everything against us. Not bad for a bunch of college players competing against a team many considered the best in the world—even if not true.

There were two interesting games. One was in Chicago, the base of operations for the Globetrotters. They wanted to put on their show but we were beating them so badly it was impossible. The people expected Hilliard to dribble and Meadowlark to make them laugh, but the college players were not co-operating. We were trying to win.

Saperstein came over to our huddle to talk with Ray Meyers, the host coach everytime the Globies played the college stars in Chicago. "The Globetrotters want to put on a show," said Abe, "and we would like your players to co-operate." We were around fifteen points in front and not anxious to act as shills for a team that had instilled animosity in us. We wanted to kill, kill, kill.

It was agreed that the College All-Stars would let the Globies stage their show as long as the score did not change. In other words, all the points scored while we were letting them produce their laughs would not count.

The show went on and I had to admit Meadowlark and the others made me laugh. The score was changing and soon it was tied. When we reached the fourth quarter we said: "Okay, turn the score back."

That was met with huge surprise. "What do you mean turn the score back?" said the official scorer. "They told us the points wouldn't count," we said. They refused to honor our request, so we went out and really whipped them for being so devious.

One night in Cincinnati, Bill Ridley of our side pulled one of the greatest and funniest plays I have ever seen. Everyone was yelling for the Globetrotters to put on their show but they couldn't because we had learned what it meant to co-operate. Someone knocked off Ridley's glasses so he couldn't see, and the fans got an unexpected show.

Ridley had to grope for the glasses while dribbling. Two Globies tried to take the ball away while Ridley did the Hilliard act. He had the ball here, there, between his legs and behind his back for about twenty-five seconds while the Globies tried to steal it. Ridley finally found his glasses and put them on, still dribbling and with three Globetrotters surrounding him.

They were furious because he had made them look foolish. As they tried to trap him, he headed for the basket. He leaped for a shot, and the Globies went up trying to cream him. Ridley spotted a trailer, so all he did was pass the ball behind his back while in the air, and the three Globetrotters were left hanging. The Globies never were funnier.

I passed up the Olympics of 1956 to play against the Globetrotters and agreed to sign with the Celtics, who drafted me. It was a matter of money plus the ridiculous mentality of the Olympic people and the AAU. I wanted to represent my country if I was guaranteed a fair opportunity to make the team, but in those years they took few college players.

Bill Russell, K. C. Jones, and Carl Cain were the only college players picked, proving I was right all along. The new Mrs. Heinsohn and her husband were not about to give up three thousand dollars from the Globies to face a stacked deck in the Olympic tryouts. At the same time, Avery Brundage, that grand old thinker from the fourteenth century, was making waves about signing letters of intent not to play professional ball.

Almost every top college basketball player intended to play in the NBA if he had the chance, and Brundage was asking them to forget it or lie about their intentions. He threatened to bar all players who didn't sign a letter of intent from the charity East-West games they were holding in Kansas City and New York.

Someone named Harry Truman handled the Kansas City problem himself. The ex-President was a Shriner, and the game was being played for the Shriners. Harry said: "Let these kids play. We're going to raise money, and don't give us any jazz about the AAU." We played in Kansas City against Russell and the other guys who were going to try out for the Olympic team.

Harry Truman saw to it that I got an AAU card that okayed my playing in Kansas City. The same players went to New York and were to play in the *Herald Tribune* Fresh Air Fund game. We all climbed aboard the same plane for New York; we practiced in New York for three days. Nothing was said about trouble with the AAU. We had our AAU cards, you know. We didn't have President Truman, though.

On Thursday night, I went home to New Jersey. On Friday morning, there were stories in the paper that certain players were not going to play in the New York charity game because they intended to participate in the Globetrotters' tour. They wanted me to sign an affidavit that I had no intention of becoming a pro, and there was no way I was going to do that.

I was committed to join the Globetrotter tour for money the day after the East-West game in the Garden, and I wasn't going to lie about it. Some signed and joined the Globetrotter tour anyway. I sat on the bench in my street clothes and watched the game because there were people in the world who were out of touch with reality. I was a pro in New York but not Kansas City. Too much.

3

I DIDN'T KNOW too much about the Boston Celtics when I was in high school. I was a Knick fan. So was my wife and whole family. I would watch the Knicks on television in the days when Joe Lapchick was the coach and they had good teams.

I had heard about Bob Cousy and this guy and that guy on the Celtics but I didn't have the vaguest idea about them. I got to know them a little better when I played ball at Holy Cross. They played a couple of exhibition games in the Worcester Auditorium and I saw Red Auerbach smoking his cigar and stomping his feet and I concluded he was a cantankerous man.

I had no reason to think of Red until my senior season, and then stories started to appear about me because of the NBA draft. In those days, they still had territorial picks that enabled a team to have automatic choice of any college player within seventy-five miles of its franchise.

Philadelphia obtained Wilt Chamberlain that way on special dispensation though he went to Kansas, because the league wanted to help owner-coach Eddie Gottlieb's weak franchise. Bill Bradley of the Knicks was the last to be drafted that way before the rule was removed. Boston had the rights to take me that way in 1956, but I wasn't sure the Celtics wanted me.

I had been prominently mentioned as an All-America that year. I had built a reputation on the East Coast somewhat like Bill Russell had on the West Coast. In those days, there was no other organized pro basketball league than the NBA. There was no ABA to outbid the NBA as it did for David Thompson with a cool three million dollars.

A ballplayer either played in the NBA or made a deal with a corporation that had a team in the AAU league. If you were white, you could play AAU ball. If you were black, you got a job with the Globetrotters. My option was the Peoria Caterpillars, a tractor outfit. They had contacted me a few weeks before my final game with Holy Cross.

I really preferred playing NBA basketball, but Peoria began getting more serious consideration when I read some of the nasty things Auerbach was saying about me in the newspapers. Let me give a few examples.

"The kid is lackadaisical. He doesn't hustle. He doesn't have the right attitude. He doesn't have the proper temperament. He isn't aggressive. He doesn't mix it up under the boards."

There wasn't much of me to like if all that were true. That kind of endorsement did not give Diane and me much to count on from the Celtics for the marriage we were planning after my graduation. I became concerned. So I went to Peoria and had an exploratory conversation with the people and proceeded to give out a propaganda story of my own.

"I have a very good offer from the AAU for a good job and some basketball," I said. "Of course, I have read the reports that Red Auerbach doesn't want me because of my temperament. I met the man for a minute about two years ago and that's the only time I ever talked to him. How he got those reports is beyond me."

I was rolling. "I'd like him," I continued, "to ask the people who know what my temperament is like. But it won't matter if I go to the AAU, and I'm very serious when I say I've given it a lot of thought. Why does he have to make statements about me when he doesn't even know me? I'd like to have the people at Holy Cross asked about my attitude in school and on the basketball court."

Red wanted to play the game, so I played the game. I hadn't made the dean's list at Holy Cross for nothing. There was nothing else I could do. It didn't matter too much by then if I played in Boston. I was intrigued by a story the Celtics might draft me and trade me to the Knicks for Ray Felix. I didn't mind playing for New York at all.

Diane and I would have been happy to go back to New York, across the river from where we grew up in New Jersey. Neither of us had a pleasant first impression of the Celtics or Red Auerbach. In fact, for many years, Diane considered Red an ogre.

She didn't like him because of all the things he said before I became a Celtic, and he did nothing to change her mind after I became a Celtic. One day early in my first season, Missy Cousy, Ginny Palazzi, and Diane decided to go into Boston to show Diane the sights. They drove in with Bob, Togo, and me and dropped us off at practice.

The girls worked their way around the stores and came back to meet us. Practice wasn't over, so they decided to go inside the Garden and wait for us. A maintenance man steered them through the dark areas and brought them to the court where we were working.

Red spotted them. He knew Mrs. Cousy and Mrs. Palazzi but not my wife. "For Chrisake!" he screamed. "Who let the broads in? No broads at practice!" Out they ran in a typical Celtic fast break.

The first thing Diane said when I saw her outside was: "Well, I met Red Auerbach." Not long after that, I took her to New York for a game, and she came looking for me in the coffee shop at our hotel. I was sitting with Red when she walked over wearing a hat she had just bought. In those days, women wore hats that they liked to have noticed.

Red noticed. "For Chrisake!" he barked, again. "You got another new hat? What are you doing? Spending all Tommy's money?" Diane was only twenty-three at the time, so she didn't really appreciate or understand that that was Red's way of making conversation. Later she learned how to handle him. Just let him growl.

Before then, she had one more example of Red's gruff sense of humor. She was pregnant for the third time and Auerbach noticed the bulge one night at a game. "For Chrisake," he said. "Are you pregnant again?" It took a long time for me to convince Diane that Red was not as bad as he acted or sounded.

It took a long time for me to convince me. If Bob Cousy had not called me one day at Holy Cross, during the time Red was turning me off about playing for the Celtics, I do not know what would have happened. I had just returned from Peoria when Cooz called.

I didn't know him at the time. I had met him only once when I was selling tickets in the Athletic Association office, a job given to me so I could earn a few dollars, and he walked in. I was introduced. He shook my hand and that was about it. I don't even think we said a word to each other until he called, I guess, by request of Red or Walter Brown, owner of the Celtics.

Cooz asked if I had had a good time in Peoria—as though anyone but Bob Haldeman could have a good time in Peoria. Then he said Walter Brown and Red wanted to talk to me. "They're interested in you," he explained. "They have some way of showing it," I said. "Forget about what you read in the papers," he said. "They are interested in you and want to see you."

I told Cooz I had no way of getting to Boston because I had no car, and he offered to drive me. I had my first real conversation with him in the car. I asked for advice. I had no idea how to handle negotiations with Red and Walter Brown. "What kinds of contract should I ask for?" I asked Cooz. "Make your own deal," he said. That was it. I was left to my own resources. There were no agents in those days to boost the prices. I had heard what some of the top forwards such as Adolph Schayes and Ed Macauley were making and judged accordingly. I was prepared to ask and fight for a nine-thousand-dollar salary when I confronted Red Auerbach for the first time.

Cousy dropped me off at the Boston Garden and I went upstairs. I was brought to Walter Brown's office and he was there with Red, though the very first thing that impressed me was the collection of bears. Walter Brown also was president of the Garden and the Boston Bruins, so people had given him all sorts of bears as gifts.

I was surrounded by bears, including what I considered at the time two of the biggest—Walter Brown and Red Auerbach. They began talking nicely, and I brought up all the nasty things I had heard. "Don't be concerned about what you read in the papers," said Red, chewing on a cigar. "We're very interested in you and don't worry about what I'm supposed to have said." Can you imagine him telling that to a referee?

I couldn't kick him out of Walter Brown's office, so I listened but wasn't ready to believe. Walter Brown then said he'd like to make a deal with me. The Celtics were ready to make me their territorial pick if I would guarantee I would play for them. I didn't know how much influence my threat of playing AAU ball had on them but, thank you, Peoria, anyway.

"That's terrific," I said after they had played their hands. "I'd like to play for Boston." They explained no one else in the NBA could take me if the Celtics wanted me, so I shouldn't go to Peoria.

We came to terms that day exactly two minutes after I stated my price, but I signed nothing. I told them I didn't want to sign a contract because I wanted to play in the two East-West All-Star games. We agreed on nine thousand dollars a year for two years. That was good money then. I was the highest-paid guy in my graduating class. I had a job right away.

I hadn't done so badly. Me against Walter Brown and Red Auerbach, and I walked away with some quick financial security for my marriage. Red and Walter Brown seemed satisfied because they were all smiles. In less than an hour, we had made a deal and there were no more hard feelings.

"Okay," Red said to me, "you're with us now, right, kid?" I nodded. "Look," he said, removing the cigar from his mouth, "I'm gonna tell you right now. Take that T-shirt you wear under your uniform and shove it. You're a Celtic now." I had always worn a T-shirt from my high school days, and that's what Red picked on as a starter.

The Auerbach full-court press was on and he never let up on me until I retired in 1965. I became his favorite whipping boy. Not right away. He was easiest on me in my rookie year until Bill Russell reported late after going to Australia for the 1956 Olympics. That was Red's system—go easy in a player's rookie year and then treat him like he belonged in his second season.

I guess Red figured I was in my second season and Russell was the rookie when he showed, so I got the treatment a little sooner. Remember, 1956–57 was the season the Celtics were going to win their first NBA championship. Bob Cousy, Bill Sharman, and Red

Auerbach never had won until I was drafted and Russell was obtained from the St. Louis Hawks for Ed Macauley and Cliff Hagan.

My shrewd mind suggested my position was a lot stronger after they had traded Macauley. The way I figured, I had to be the big scoring forward with Easy Ed gone. In the meantime, I had played well in a game against the Globetrotters that Auerbach and Walter Brown had seen in the Boston Garden.

I hadn't signed my contract yet, so I went to see Walter Brown about an adjustment. Fortunately, Red was back home in Washington, otherwise I probably would have wound up with less money. I explained to Walter that my situation had changed because I was going to replace Macauley, a star in the league. I asked if there was a chance for a bonus in my second year if I did well in my first.

He asked how much I was thinking about. I told him in the neighborhood of two thousand dollars. He said fine and wrote it into the contract. I didn't see Auerbach all summer. He was down at Kutsher's in the Catskills, playing poker and tennis. The next time I saw him was at training camp and he said nothing about the raise I had gotten out of Walter Brown, though I had to wait a year for it.

Money was not on Red's mind at that time, anyway. He was thinking of torture. Not just for me but for all the poor souls invited into his horror chamber. Our training camp was at the Boston Arena, where the steps were high and plentiful. You cracked one joke or laughed a little and you would run all the steps. Since I had a sense of humor, I ran the steps more than anyone.

Red was supposed to have been in the Navy during World War II, but the Celtics were convinced he had been a Marine drill sergeant at Parris Island. He ran a camp like he was getting us ready to storm Iwo Jima rather than Fort Wayne or Minneapolis. I found out why in my first game against the Knicks.

It was in Madison Square Garden. I got into the pivot and cut off Ray Felix; he stuck his knee out, and I had a charley horse in the right leg. In the second quarter, I got into the pivot and cut the other way; he stuck his knee out, and I had a charley horse in the other leg. I had only played a half and I had run out of legs.

Auerbach was aware that rookies in the NBA had to prove they were tough enough to survive. Joe Lapchick had a quaint way of putting it. "They ask you the question in this league," he said, "and if you don't come up with the right answer, you're in trouble."

Felix was one of those who asked me the question in my first season. Ray was a big, awkward fellow but not shy when it came to throwing punches. He and Russell once staged the world's tallest fight in the first game of a doubleheader at Syracuse. I had the rematch with Ray in the second part of a doubleheader in Madison Square Garden.

I think I landed a right to Ray's armpit and he missed me with a hook before they broke it up. It was a rougher league when I first came into it. Now they jump over a player under the boards. Vern Mikkelsen of the Lakers and Joe Graboski of Philadelphia, the first schoolboy to play in the league, would go through you. It was all muscle.

I remember Auerbach telling me how to play Mikkelsen. "He can't shoot outside," said Red. "He's got a lousy two-hand shot. Let him shoot the outside shot and then block him off the boards."

A very simple instruction. Mikkelsen got out there, I backed off him five feet, he shot the two-hand set and missed it. I turned and stood there to block him off the boards. Meanwhile, he's 230 and coming at me. He didn't go around, he went through my back and came out the front. He shoved me so hard, my sneakers burned.

For this test of strength and courage, Auerbach prepared me by insisting I play under 220. I was 235 my last season at Holy Cross, but Red wanted me slimmer for quickness, or it might have been his way to get even with the Germans. There was no doubt in my mind I needed more strength when I had to handle the muscle of an Ed Kalafat, mean down to his name.

There was no time to consider maintaining weight in the camp Auerbach ran and ran and ran. He must have had a deal with the guy selling sneakers to the Celtics the way he ran us. We scrimmaged twice a day. We had 2½-hour practices and never stood still. We ran all the time. No water, nothing.

The training period then was almost six weeks, so there was plenty of time for Red to enjoy himself. His pet idea for getting us in shape was three-on-three full-court games, losers stay on. That was after the wind sprints, the scrimmages, and running the stairs. He got us so agitated, we had fights among ourselves on the court.

Heinsohn, of course, was Red's whipping boy, so I ran until my hair hung—and I always had a crew cut. He made sure I would be out there for at least five games. The fix was in. He would give me two teammates that would guarantee I'd lose. Red was funny that way.

He would call all the fouls and settle all arguments. He would push me until everyone got a pain in the side from laughing at my predicament. He pushed me because he somehow knew I could be pushed without breaking—too much.

One day I had been on the court for four games and I was dead tired. I drove for what would be the winning basket, but Dan Swartz fouled me and Red refused to call it. If the other team scored, it would be all over and I would have to go for another game. I had to do something fast.

Someone grabbed the rebound on my shot and pitched it out to Ron Bonham. I took three steps up the court and tackled him like he was a broken-field runner. He was a rookie at the time. He couldn't believe what had just happened until he got to know Auerbach and me a lot better.

Red was marvelous at handling people. That was his strength. He knew how to motivate players as well as blend twelve personalities into a team effort. That's an art. Some say there is only one way a coach can handle players. That's ridiculous. Auerbach had twelve different ways for twelve different players.

I remember when John Havlicek first came to the Celtics. He was a rookie, so Red treated him sweet and lovely. Such a nice guy. The only thing Havlicek was asked to do was carry the basketballs, as do all rookies on all teams.

Auerbach never raised his voice to Havlicek until the first game of his second season. Hondo was one of Red's favorite players from the time he scouted him at Ohio State. He saw things in Havlicek few people detected, which was another one of Red's strengths and explains why the Celtics always managed to get Celtic-type players.

I know someone spread a story that Red supposedly did not want to draft Havlicek but Walter Brown insisted on it. That someone didn't like Auerbach and was trying to demean him. The guy claimed he was there and heard the conversation, but it just wasn't true. Red was a Havlicek man from the word go.

We were playing the first game of the 1963–64 season and Havlicek had shown he could fill the sixth-man role since Frank Ramsey, the greatest of them all, had retired. We went to the dressing room at half time and John was relaxing on his stool. Red had never criticized him. It had been total encouragement up to that point.

"Havlicek!" screamed Red, shaking the walls. "You were terrible. What the hell are you doing out there?" Auerbach climbed all over him. Havlicek, after a year of being nothing but the greatest, never having had his name mentioned in a critical manner, was shell-shocked. He couldn't have been more disturbed if someone had stolen his hair drier.

I looked at him and he was looking for a place to hide. "This man's yelling at me," he said, increduously. "This man's yelling at me." I told him to relax. I told him he was a rookie last year and Red doesn't yell at rookies. "You're a sophomore now," I said, "and you're gonna take it like everyone else."

Auerbach had a way of goading and berating his players that they accepted. I believe he was dealing with a different brand of players in those days. I don't think he could do that now with the modern types. They are too sensitive and independent. They would sulk and rebel. They would count their money and say: "Who is he to talk that way to me?"

Red established attitudes and images that lasted for years. Me, for example. Some of the things Auerbach said to me in the dressing room leaked to newspapermen and I've been a shnook to many of them to this day. They couldn't understand why Red used me as a whipping boy and why I tolerated it. They never got to know the real Tommy Heinsohn.

I assume they expected me to pack my socks and jocks and take the next bus to Peoria. They never understood that Auerbach knew I had the personality and the patience to take his well-calculated abuse without considering it too personal. I had as big an ego as anyone, but Red discovered quickly that I was less sensitive and more tolerant than the others and less likely to be neurotic about criticism.

It is important for a coach to have someone on the team he can kid and abuse to get the message across to the others. Willis Reed served that purpose for Red Holzman on the Knicks during their winning years. Red knew he could scream at Willis not to turn his head on defense and to get back in a hurry without a serious problem.

Reed was the captain and Holzman used him to create respect and unity of purpose by treating him less favorably than the others. I don't care if you are on a winning or losing team, players lose respect for a coach who caters to certain individuals unless they understand the reason.

It's well known that Jim Loscutoff was thinking of justifiable homicide at one time. That's when he was in rehabilitation from a slipped disc in his back and Red had him diving for basketballs in training camp to test it. Cruel, maybe, if you did not understand that Auerbach was trying to re-establish confidence in Loscy because the doctors had said he might never play again.

You seldom appreciate what people have done for you until you look back years later. Of course, I did a lot for Auerbach, as well as myself, that first year in the NBA and for many years. It did no harm to the Celtic situation when I played well enough to make the All-Star game in my rookie year.

That was the game in which Bill Sharman indicated he might have invested his time better as a pitcher rather than an outfielder in the Brooklyn Dodgers' chain. He threw a pass to Bob Cousy that wound up as a seventy-foot basket. Some arm.

I also earned Rookie-of-the-Year honors as well as my nickname Ack-Ack because some thought I shot too much. I think it was Leonard Koppett, then with the New York *Post,* who was responsible for the name by suggesting I even shot while sitting on the bench. My good friend Cousy certainly didn't help influence anyone that I could pass the ball as well as any forward.

"Hey, look at this," said Cooz in the dressing room after the East beat the West, 109–97, in the game played at the Boston Garden. "Heinsohn took twenty-two shots. That's a lot for a corner man on this team. We might have to have a meeting on this." He never stopped needling me about being a gunner.

Though it wasn't necessarily so, I had to be funny about it because that was my nature. I said that the only time I shot the ball was when it touched my hands. One night in Cincinnati I scored in the first three seconds. The same game I hit ten baskets in the third quarter, proving I could shoot from anywhere at any time but still no reason for people to assume I never passed. Was it?

One reason I acquired a reputation for not passing was because of the way Cousy handled the ball. He would give it to you in perfect shooting position, and Auerbach insisted you take the shot when you had it. Also, the guys would always unload the ball on me when the clock was running out because they knew I would get the shot off somehow, somewhere.

I gave the fans a wonderful opportunity to draw their own conclusions by being one of the few Celtics to start from my first day with the team. My first game was an exhibition against the Knicks, and I took a hook shot from the dressing room. "Are you kidding?" said Dick McGuire, a conservative two-hand set shooter Ned Irish once offered ten dollars a shot to shoot, but McGuire didn't earn an extra nickel in the game. "You can't get away with that stuff in this league."

I told Dickie he hadn't seen anything yet. He never forgot that. Me, a rookie, popping off like that in his first exhibition game. He went home and told his wife, Terry: "There's a kid on the Celtics who is the cockiest kid I've ever seen."

McGuire was right in two respects. I was confident. Also, I didn't get away with that stuff in the league. Not for long, anyway. Only from 1956 to 1965, during which time the Celtics failed to win the title only once. My arm went before my legs.

4

I STILL REMEMBER a story the late Al Hirshberg wrote in a magazine. Al was a Boston sportswriter who was responsible for *Fear Strikes Out,* a book then a movie about Jimmy Piersall, the Boston Red Sox outfielder.

"Some people are calling the Celtics the greatest basketball squad ever assembled," he wrote just before we won our first championship in 1957. Greater than the 1949–54 Minneapolis Lakers with George Mikan. Coach Red Auerbach conceded that Boston's long years of basketball frustration might at last be over.

"This club at full strength is an answer to a coach's dream," said Red. "We've got that same great backcourt strength we've always had with Cousy and Sharman. We're stronger than we've ever been up front and we've got good depth everywhere. Heinsohn and Loscutoff are powerfully built boys who can get rebounds, and Russell is going to be the best center in the business, if he isn't already. I never saw anyone do what he did—come in at midseason, with no experi-

ence, no training, and no knowledge of the league, and take right
over."

"Auerbach, Cousy, and Macauley all arrived on the scene seven
years ago," continued Hirshberg in his perceptive article written during the 1956–57 season. "Sharman got there one year later. Year
after year, the Celtics were knocked out of the playoffs early. Cousy,
a master ballhandler and playmaker, was the league's showiest per-
former, and Macauley one of the leading scorers. Sharman was one
of the best set shots and one of the most successful foul shooters of
modern times."

It all added up to a team that was to dominate the NBA for
years. It was a team that through the years was to play and fight
together—right down to the coach. I remember a night we had to
grab big Neil Johnston, coach of the Philadelphia Warriors, because
he wanted to swing at Auerbach, who wanted to swing at Neil. Then
there was the time Richie Guerin, in his rookie year with the Knicks,
pushed Sharman a little too far. You had to know Sharman to appreciate how tough he was because he rarely showed his emotions.

Sharman was like a treacherous bulldog that would suddenly
bite and refuse to let go. You spelled his name T-E-N-A-C-I-O-U-S.
He was not a gifted player. He didn't have speed. He couldn't jump.
He wasn't as smooth or graceful as Cousy. All he could do was play
basketball.

He could put the ball in the basket. They mention K. C. Jones
as the perfect example of a defensive guard, but Sharman played defense as well and maybe even better. Bill didn't have the quickness
but he intimidated his man. He played him in his socks. He picked
him up and stayed with him all the way to his girlfriend's apartment.

Sharman used to drive Carl Braun out of his mind. Braun was
one of the NBA's finest shooters but often went away from his
strength to engage Bill in the manly art of self-defense. Carl was no
fighter, so he did not represent a fair test of Sharman's ability to handle himself.

Guerin was something else. He was a knothead like Sharman.
He had just gotten out of the Marines, and you didn't fool around
with Richie Guerin, though he was a rookie as I was when we played
the Knicks an exhibition game in New Haven.

A fight started and Richie injured his hand with a punch to the
side of Sharman's head. That ended the fight quickly, but not for

Sharman. He couldn't wait to get even for Guerin's audaciousness. If I recall correctly, Bill got his chance in the game at Madison Square Garden when Ray Felix hurt both my legs.

Sharman had an explosive temper. He was like the guys in the movies who swallow the chemical in the tube and turn from Dr. Jekyll to Mr. Hyde before your eyes. When he saw Guerin again, it was like saying "Bill Russell" to Wilt Chamberlain. In no time, Sharman knocked Richie out and was banging his head on the floor when three of us dragged Bill away.

It's funny because Sharman gave the impression he was a sweet, lovable person who wouldn't say a nasty word, even to a referee or Auerbach, unless something triggered him. Since he was often in Red's company, that was not difficult. One word of criticism from Auerbach, and Sharman would bristle like a porcupine.

That was the signal to move away. Auerbach had a tougher time getting along with Sharman than anyone because of Bill's personality. Red couldn't and wouldn't say one word to him, which was a drastic change in Red's personality. He just had to leave Bill alone.

There was no one more dedicated to winning than Sharman. There was no one more dedicated to perfection than Sharman—even more so than Cousy, who had total impatience with other people's mistakes and his own. Bill was a pill-taker. He had special diets. He was exact. He had to have a cup of tea at precisely two minutes after ten and had to do special exercises ten minutes before every game.

We would all be sitting at our stalls and Sharman would stretch out on the floor and do his exercises. He still believes in exercises. He had Chamberlain and the Lakers doing them before they left the dressing room. Auerbach, of course, let Sharman lay on the floor and do what he pleased.

Red recognized he had people with strong personalities and egos. He let Cousy run the fast break his way after they had a long period of personal adjustments when Cooz first came to the Celtics. Red let Russell do his thing on the court, with the media, and not sign autographs because there were more important things to consider if he wanted a winning situation.

That's why Red stroked Frank Ramsey, a most sensitive individual, who broke down when criticized. The story has been told many times but is worth repeating how Ramsey cried in the locker room after his first losing game with the Celtics.

Ed Macauley asked why he was crying. "This is the first time I ever lost a game," sobbed Ramsey. "You're going to lose a lot of games in the pros," suggested Macauley. "Well," said Frank, "it ain't gonna make me cry any less."

Ramsey used better grammar, but I'm only repeating a conversation I was told occurred before I became a Celtic. It does reflect Frank's sensitivity and emotion. I don't think Ramsey had the greatest skills in the world or even the NBA. But he was smart. He did the little and big things that helped you win.

He was by far the greatest sixth man to ever play pro basketball. He was overshadowed by everybody. Russell, Cousy, Sharman, and me, ultimately. But he was as fine a ballplayer as anyone on the team. He had a dramatic impact on any game within the first fifteen seconds after he came off the bench. That was a special talent.

John Havlicek is a better basketball player than Ramsey and also was an outstanding sixth man until Auerbach was forced to start him after losing Sam Jones and K. C. Jones. But to pick a team up right away coming off the bench, Ramsey was the greatest. He would sometimes play six-eleven guys like Nate Thurmond. Red, consequently, always puffed Ramsey because he knew if it was otherwise, Frank would melt like the first snow of spring.

Ramsey had other dimensions. He was a nit-picker. He was conservative by philosophy and dress. He was money-oriented and got his biggest thrills finding loopholes in tax laws. He was a shrewd businessman and ultimately became wealthy. He always was thinking money.

Once he flew to Washington on our way to playing at the University of Maryland fieldhouse. Frank was sitting next to me on the plane, and behind us was someone and his attorney apparently on their way to the Internal Revenue Service to defend a tax position.

They were in a deep conversation about tax strategy for the review. I was reading a book, but as soon as Ramsey heard IRS and loopholes, he pushed his seat back to create an opening for him to eavesdrop. It was like that E. F. Hutton television commercial.

Frank stuck his ear to the crack while the two fellows went on and on. He kept nudging me and saying: "Listen to this. Listen to this." He was in ecstasy. I could have cared less, but that was the kind of person he was when it came to money and other small things.

He was meticulous down to the clothes he wore. Everyone came to practice with leisure slacks and shirts. Not Mr. Ramsey. He always wore a jacket, button-down shirt, and tie, as though ready to go to the bank.

That gave me the inspiration for a practical joke. Ramsey, you see, was a practical joker himself, and I was his target. It developed into a running thing between us. He was an avid reader, so whenever he put his book down on the plane to visit the watershed, I'd reach over and rip out the last chapter. I don't think he ever found out who got the girl or committed the murder.

His idea of a big joke was to scheme with Cousy and Buddy Leroux, the trainer, to get me fined by Auerbach for being late to practice. Cousy, my chauffeur, would grab an extra cup of coffee, and Leroux would tape my ankles slowly just to delay me. Ramsey would stand at the head of the stairs and yell: "Red! Red! He's four minutes late! That's a dollar! Make him pay the dollar, Red!"

One day I had a long talk with Frank. I told him I knew what he and the others were doing and suggested he get off me. "What do you mean?" he said, feigning surprise. "You can't walk in late all the time and expect us to wait for you."

I advised him not to be my keeper. "I'm going to do what I have to do," he said, carrying it to the ultimate. He was having a great laugh at my expense. So I devised a campaign just for him. I'd fix him for this: "Red! Red! He's four minutes late!"

Frank would come into the locker room, remove his jacket, and hang it up. Now, most people wearing a button-down shirt wouldn't yank out the tie. Frank was meticulous, remember? He unbuttoned the two buttons first, took off the tie and hung it up, then took off the shirt. He went through the ritual every day.

Normal people just didn't do that, but Frank was different. His shoes always were immaculately shined and he would put them down perfectly parallel near his locker. He wasn't the most stylish individual, but everything had to be just right.

For three full weeks, four or five practice sessions each week, I waited until he hung up his clothes and left. Then I took a razor blade and cut one of the buttons three quarters of the way through before I went upstairs to practice. Sure enough, Frank would be there chirping: "Red! Red! He's four minutes late!"

After working out, Ramsey would take a shower, slip into his pants, put his shoes and socks on and his shirt, work the tie into place, and go to button the buttons, and one would come off in his hand. "I got to get that Jean to fix these buttons," he would say, referring to his wife.

The next day I did something else. I cut one of his shoelaces three quarters of the way through. He would put on the shoe, yank the lace, and it would snap. "Oh, gee," he'd say while tieing a knot. Then I would go back to the button and he would go through the same routine.

For a change of pace, I would take his belt and force the metal prong that fits into the holes through the other side so it didn't work. He'd get dressed and couldn't buckle his belt. One day the button, one day the lace, one day the belt. He never suspected a thing for three weeks.

Finally, one day in the dressing room he came over to me. "Hawk," he said, "are you doing these things to me?" I indicated I didn't know what he was talking about. "Hawk," he said, "let's have a truce." I said: "What do you mean, a truce? I'm not doing anything to you. What kind of a truce would you want? Are you doing something to me? Are you bothering me in some way?" I won that one by default.

Ramsey would play jokes on everybody, especially when he had vulnerable people such as Togo Palazzi and Gene Conley, the big pitcher. Conley was a nice guy and would believe anything. He was drafted out of Washington State by the Celtics and played in the 1952–53 season before the Braves insisted he give up basketball to concentrate on baseball.

Gene eventually came back to the Celtics and played from 1958–63 and finished with the Knicks. Besides being a powerful man, he had a certain innocence that got him involved in strange happenings. One time, for example, when he was with the Knicks and still living in the Boston area, he went out to LaGuardia by himself to catch a late plane after the Celtics had won in the Garden.

Conley walked over to the luggage area to check his bag, and a porter recognized him. They talked about the beating the Celtics had just given the Knicks. "We're going to bomb Boston tomorrow night," said Gene, meaning the rematch in the Boston Garden, of course.

Someone overheard the remark and, not knowing Conley, reported it to airport security. The next thing you know, the police picked up Gene and took him to the FBI office. After three hours of questioning and many phone calls to Garden officials, Gene finally convinced the law he had meant the Knicks were going to bomb the Celtics. That didn't happen, either, by the way.

Conley was a perfect pigeon for Ramsey. We were on a plane one day going to Cincinnati, and they began serving cocktail sandwiches. Conley was very hungry. He hadn't eaten all day. When he saw the size of the sandwiches, he got up and asked the guys if they wanted their sandwiches, and they told him they did.

He went back to his seat starved. Ramsey, sitting directly in front of Gene, leaned back and pointed to a woman across the aisle. "That woman over there," he said to Conley, "just asked if I wanted her sandwiches. Apparently she doesn't want them."

Conley sat back, reached across the aisle, and plucked the sandwiches off her tray. She turned, and he was just about to thank her when she screamed: "What are you doing? Who do you think you are, taking my sandwiches like that?"

That upset Conley, and he admonished Ramsey for embarrassing him that way. Frank apologized and promised never to do it again. We got off the plane and headed through the airport, and Conley couldn't find the men's room.

Whom did he ask? Ramsey, of course. Frank pointed at a door. "Go through that door there," Conley was told. Gene walked through and wound up smack in the ladies' room.

Ramsey moved to the luggage area laughing so hard, he was crying. He saw Conley coming and started running. They ran outside the building and four times around the quadrangle at the Cincinnati airport before Gene gave up.

Maybe the most intricate joke Ramsey's impish mind ever devised was the one he pulled on Palazzi, another lovable but naïve individual. I knew Togo from Union City and Holy Cross and followed him to the Celtics by two seasons. I was actually with him only about six months in Boston before he was traded to Syracuse, but I could fill a book with Togo Palazzi stories.

We were at the Minneapolis airport waiting for a charter flight to another exhibition game, and Ramsey went to a row of phone booths. He checked the number in one and walked to the far end and called the booth. Someone on the team answered and said: "Togo, it's for you."

Togo grabbed the phone. Ramsey disguised his voice and said: "Togo Palazzi. This is Joe Samford. I've sworn out a warrant for your arrest for attacking my wife last night." That wasn't the name Ramsey used, but it was so long ago, for the sake of the story, let's say it was Samford.

"Waddya mean attacking your wife last night?" said Togo, slightly startled. "I don't know anyone in Minneapolis, I'm married and don't go out with anyone, and you're telling me I attacked your wife? You're crazy."

That didn't stop Ramsey. "The police would like to see you," he said to Togo from his booth about ten yards away. "They want to talk to you. I understand you're leaving because I called your hotel, so wait there for the police because they don't want any problems."

Togo came out of the booth shaking. The guys were playing cards but Ramsey had alerted everyone, so they knew what was going on. "Gee," said Togo, "a guy just called me. He's gotten a warrant for my arrest for attacking his wife. What the hell is that?"

Everyone played dumb. Then something dawned on Togo. "It must be one of you guys," he said. "Now I know. It was one of you guys." He sat in a chair and relaxed. Ramsey wasn't through. He never gave up that easily.

It happened that we were traveling with the Minneapolis Lakers on the same charter. Frank walked over to Clyde Lovellette, another guy with a cute sense of humor, and told him the story. He gave Clyde the phone number of the first booth and told him to go the other end and call from there, making believe he was the chief of police.

The phone rang, again, and someone picked it up. "Togo," he announced, "there's another call for you. He says he's the chief of police." Togo looked at us and laughed. "Do you think I'm a fool?" he said.

Nobody blinked. He started to count Celtics, accounting for all of us including Ramsey. He didn't count Lakers and had no idea Lovellette was on the other phone this time, posing as Chief Jones or something. "I want you to wait by the police booth for my arrival," Clyde told him.

Togo emerged from the booth looking sick. First it was the husband and then the chief of police. "What are they talking about?" he said, talking to himself. "I'm in my room, I did nothing. That was the police chief. He's got a warrant for my arrest." He was hooked.

Five minutes went by and then Ramsey sneaked over to the ticket agent and asked him to make an announcement. A few seconds later this was heard: "Togo Palazzi! Togo Palazzi! Please report to Chief Jones at the police information booth in the main lobby of the airport."

Togo picked up his bag, leaped over the railing, and ran onto the plane. He hid in the can until everyone got on board. When they locked the doors, Togo came out and the plane took off. He was safe, finally. That's what he thought.

Ramsey went up front to the cabin. He talked the pilot into interrupting the music for a news bulletin. "We interrupt this program for a special new bulletin," said the pilot, simulating a newscaster. "Togo Palazzi, basketball star of the Boston Celtics, is being sought for the attack of Joe Samford's wife last night in Minneapolis. He was nearly apprehended at the airport and is currently flying on to St. Louis. Police authorities will be waiting at the airport with extradition papers to bring him back from St. Louis."

Togo began looking for a parachute. He was ready to bail out. Auerbach finally told him it was all a joke. Togo's reaction? "It can't be," he said to Red. "They wouldn't do anything like that to me." No way.

That should give you an idea as to the characters who made up the Celtics. They were the people Auerbach used to build a championship in my first season. They made us laugh and a lot of other people cry, including me. For example, there never will be anything like the final game of my first championship, which wound up with me crying.

5

A TIME-OUT WAS called. We were leading the St. Louis Hawks 103–101, and the Boston Celtics were only thirteen seconds away from their first world championship. Cousy had one more foul shot coming when play resumed, and everyone knew how he responded to pressure.

Cooz had made the first quite calmly before St. Louis asked for time. There was no doubt he would make the second. No doubt in our huddle, anyway. Red went through the whole routine. "Now when Cousy makes the foul," he said, taking that for granted, "no fouls. We're ahead by three and we can give them the basket."

Nobody noticed Cousy standing off on the side by himself. He wasn't in the huddle. Auerbach reviewed the game situation and what to do and what not to do, figuring Cooz surely would make the shot. I figured the same as we lined up along the foul line.

I assumed my position. I got down and coiled and prepared to beat my man into the lane. It was a matter of timing and watching the shooter's knees. When his knees came up, I jumped into the lane for a tip-in if the shot was missed.

I didn't expect any rebound with Cousy shooting at a time when one more point would move the game out of reach. I went through my routine, anyway. I watched Cousy bounce the ball while getting ready to shoot. I looked his way, again, and I saw his knees bend—knees straighten.

I crashed, looking for the ball. No ball. There's no ball! Cousy took the shot and it went three feet out of his hands. He didn't even hit the rim. I couldn't believe it. Could you imagine the great Bob Cousy missing a foul shot by so much in a situation such as that?

Were Cousy, Sharman, and Auerbach destined to be denied, again, after reaching the seventh game of the final playoffs? Were all those games of the regular season and the playoffs with Syracuse to be wasted? Had Auerbach's fist fight with Ben Kerner, owner of the Hawks, been for nothing?

The whole season had been dedicated to winning a championship for Boston, Auerbach, Cousy, and Sharman. It didn't take long to learn the history of the Celtics when I put on the uniform that season. It didn't take Bill Russell long to realize what the title meant to Red, Cousy, and Sharman after he joined us in December to play forty-eight of the seventy-two games.

In those days, there were only eight teams in the NBA, and the rivalries were more intense and eventful. Teams would play each other more often and had less time to forget about the last fight. In 1956, my rookie year, until I retired in 1965, the Knicks were in a state of decline, so there wasn't too much excitement or prestige playing and beating them.

Syracuse and Philadelphia were the other cities and teams in the East. I would have to say that Syracuse represented the most traumatic experience for the Celtics—whether we went there or the Nationals played at our place. The Nats had a reputation for fighting that originated in the days when coach Al Cervi was the fight promoter until Paul Seymour took the job as player-coach.

Syracuse was the acknowledged snake pit of the league. Everything seemed to happen when you visited there. This was before my time, but they tell me a little old lady would sit in the front row with an umbrella and threaten the referees with it. I think she must have willed a couple of seats to her two daughters because there always were two fat girls in the same area who never let up on me or the referees.

Syracuse was the place where John Nucatola, now supervisor of officials, received some strange advice on his first visit. "Look," said the referee with whom he was working, "you watch the clock. When it gets to ten seconds to go, forget about the game. Run for the dressing room."

Then there was Charley Eckman, a colorful referee who later was to be picked by owner Fred Zollner to coach the Ft. Wayne Pistons. One night Charley was working the final game of what was to be a Knicks' elimination from the playoffs by the Nats. Those were the days of Ernie Vandeweghe, Dick McGuire, Carl Braun, Vince Boryla, and Sweetwater Clifton—when the Knicks had teams that made the playoffs every year.

That series turned out to be unusually wild. One time, the basket shook while Boryla was shooting a foul. Joe Lapchick complained that a youngster had his foot against the support and was causing the backboard to sway. Joe was told the overhead air vent was causing the problem. "How come it's not moving at their end?" said Lapchick, pointing to the vent over the other basket.

Well, the final game ended and the Knicks lost. Two policemen rushed onto the floor to escort Eckman and the other official to the dressing room. Too late. A blurred figure dashed past the cops as Charley ran for the street and safety. He never waited around for a shower or to confront Syracuse justice that was reserved for basketball enemies.

For some reason, whenever we played Syracuse, I got into a fuss with Paul Seymour. For some reason, it always turned out the same way. Identical results three different times, and that was long before instant replays.

One time he was a player, and on the other occasions he was coach of the Syracuse team. Seymour was a guard and Cervi, the coach, had a play where Paul would drive the basket, flip the ball over his shoulder to Schayes, and then pick off Dolph's man. That would release Schayes for his best shot—a two-hand set.

Seymour was adept at blocking for Dolph and, on our team, Auerbach was furious whenever a big man was picked by a small guard. His reasoning was a good big man never should be intimidated by a good small man. I sometimes wondered when he told us that whether he was aware of the double standard he was advancing when he, the good small man, intimidated me, the good big man who towered over him.

There were constant reminders in our huddles that we must make the man who blocked for Schayes pay the price. In Auerbach's mind that ranged from asking him to politely step aside so you could get at Dolph to hitting him so hard he would have to pay to get back into the arena. Since I happened to guard Schayes most of the time, Mr. Auerbach, obviously, said all those things for my benefit.

One night in Syracuse, I finally remembered I had to hit Seymour if only to impress Auerbach. So when Paul pulled his pet play for Schayes, I plowed into Seymour, knocked him down, and stepped on him to make sure Red would be satisfied.

It was so obvious, the referee called it a two-shot foul, which they did in those days when it was considered deliberate or flagrant. I wanted to make sure Paul got the message so I wouldn't have to be too physical with him in the future. He had a message for me, which I began to detect when Johnny Kerr and some other guy each grabbed my arms and one wrapped an arm around my neck.

They held me and waited for Seymour to get even. Paul, furious, couldn't wait. He came off the floor with his crew cut bristling. He rushed at me and reached way back for his best swing. As he was throwing the punch, he slipped and fell.

His momentum carried him headlong into me. All I could do under the circumstances was lift my knee in self-defense because of the two bullies holding me. Seymour's jaw hit my knee and he was knocked out.

When he regained consciousness and found out what had happened, he was embarrassed and angrier. Ballplayers do not forget such things, especially when that player is Seymour, never known to turn away from a fight.

He had to wait awhile to get even but it was inevitable, because when our teams played each other it was like rubbing two redwoods together—a huge fire resulted. It didn't matter whether the less menacing Cousy or the awesome Loscutoff was involved in a fight, Paul apparently had arranged for two of his bouncers to grab me as soon as something broke out.

I don't know who was in the next fight but, sure enough,

Seymour's designated holders tied me up. The action was about twenty feet away, but they held me and Paul, who was the coach then, came running off the bench. He couldn't wait to throw the punch. It was his turn in the batting cage.

He was prepared to knock me out of the ball park. He tore at me, slipped again, banged his jaw against my knee again, and was knocked out again. The next season the same thing happened. Three times he never hit me with a punch, and every time he was knocked out by my knee. He was in a terrible rut.

He finally gave up. I think the two designated holders got tired of watching the same act. Normally, NBA fights are flash things that are ignited by the contact and emotion and are quickly forgotten. Not Seymour. He was one of the few players who would never talk to me off the court. He would see me coming and go the other way. I wonder why?

They weren't the least bit bashful in Syracuse. If the players weren't in the mood to fight, the fans were prepared to be accommodating. The idea when you played on the road in those days was not only to win, but survive as well, especially in Syracuse. There was this playoff game in March of 1961, and everyone in the Onondaga County War Memorial Auditorium was more charged up than usual. Suddenly a fan appeared in our huddle during a time-out and began swinging.

Nobody bothered to ask why. He was passed around once Auerbach put him in motion. I never was near the guy as the huddle closed on him. Conley and Loscutoff double-teamed him. One hit him in the stomach and the other straightened him up. They repeated the process several times.

Someone then hit the poor guy so hard, he rocketed out of the huddle like an antiballistic missile and flew across the floor. He actually hit his head on the basket support, which was how far he traveled.

That started a riot for some reason. People came out of the stands. I don't have to tell you how the Syracuse papers carried on about that. We won and left town, anyway, so we forgot about it until our first game back there the following season.

We arrived in town for a Thursday game not knowing that the previous day a $750,000 damage suit had been filed by three

Syracuse fans—the guy in the huddle and two others charging assault and battery in the riot that followed. I had never touched anyone, but I was one of the named players.

They were suing Auerbach, the Celtics, the NBA, the arena, the county, Frank Ramsey, Conley, Loscutoff, and Heinsohn. They stopped at President Kennedy, obviously. I was included because I had the reputation for being a fighter, and it was assumed, if there was a fight in Syracuse, I had to be involved. I never even got a swing at the guy in our huddle. I would have, quite frankly, if I had been close enough to him.

We had arrived at our hotel around four in the morning after a charter flight from somewhere. About nine, there was a knock on my door. I was rooming with Carl Braun, who was spending his final NBA season with the Celtics after many years with the Knicks as player and one as coach. I asked who it was. I heard someone mumbling at the door.

Carl and I had been asleep and out of it when this happened. "Who is it?" I yelled. More mumbling. I figured it must be one of the guys from Holy Cross who lived in the area and had come over to see me. I got out of bed, opened the door, and there was a guy with a white piece of paper, a woman, and a photographer.

"Are you Tommy Heinsohn?" asked the guy with the paper. I nodded and he said: "This is for you." He extended the paper. It registered somewhere in the depths of my foggy mind that you have to accept a subpoena for it to be legally served. I refused to take it from him. I wouldn't let him touch me with it, and I did not invite him into the room.

He figured he would outsmart me, so he threw the paper into the room and it hit the floor. Braun was snuggled on his pillow, with the blanket over his head, not aware of what was going on. "Carl! Carl!" I yelled. "Get up! Throw it out of the room! Quick! Throw it out of the room!"

Carl and the blankets flew out of bed. I pointed to the paper on the floor. "Get it out, Carl!" I shouted. "Throw it out of the room!" I didn't want to touch the subpoena and I wanted Carl to toss it out before the guy slammed the door.

He ran, picked up the paper, and was about to throw it through the open door when they snapped his picture. I at least slept in my undershorts. The got a picture of a naked Carl Braun holding the subpoena, but he was too bewildered to notice it.

"What the hell was that all about?" he said as his head began to clear. "Have you been messing around with someone's wife or something?" What could I tell him? I quickly called Auerbach and informed him of the subpoena. He figured out right away that it was for the fight we had during the playoffs that actually had started when Red protested a goaltending call against Russell.

They took all kinds of depositions for a whole year and, according to the testimony, not one Celtic admitted he was in a fight. Loscutoff hadn't done a thing. Ramsey never had lifted a hand. Conley, gone by then and playing for the New York Tuckers in the American Basketball League, was not asked to testify. Cousy, who had sneaked in a few shots in the huddle, escaped the lawsuit because everyone knew he abhorred violence.

I had played the role of a fighter so often, I was a fighter even when I didn't fight. That's what happens when you are typecast. I'm sure Raquel Welch knows what I mean, and if she doesn't, I'd be happy to explain at her convenience.

They settled the lawsuit, ultimately, for a roll of quarters and, I think, an autographed picture of me showing my knee to Seymour. Under those conditions, you can appreciate what it meant whenever or wherever the Celtics and Nationals met to sweat. Which brings me back to my first playoffs and my first championship in my first season.

Look in the record book and you will see: 1955 playoffs, Celtics eliminated by Syracuse in Eastern Conference final; 1956 playoffs, Celtics eliminated by Syracuse in Eastern Conference semifinal. Add the normal team attitudes before and after I joined the Celtics to the growing frustrations of Auerbach, Sharman, and Cousy because they had not won a title and you appreciate what it meant to eliminate the Nats, 3–0, and qualify to play St. Louis for the 1957 championship.

Cousy said some nice things about me after we had taken the first one from Syracuse, 108–90. About my defense against Schayes, not the eight baskets I made on twenty-one shots. "We had Dolph in check all night," said Cooz. "He only scored three baskets. Auerbach had Heinsohn chasing him all over the court. The big job that

Tommy did was to keep Schayes from shooting outside. That he did like the great pro that he is."

Strange Cooz didn't say a word about my great defense after Schayes hit thirty-one in the second game we won, 120–105, up in the snake pit. Of course, I got back thirty, so it wasn't a total loss. But those things were insignificant compared to the tension that was building inside Auerbach, Cousy, and Sharman as we moved closer to the final playoffs.

It manifested itself in obvious ways with Red and Cooz, while Sharman by nature was able to bury it deeper. A clock broke down in the third period of the second game with the score tied. Auerbach and Seymour went to the desk to protect their coaching interests from each other and were on the verge of throwing punches when Heinsohn the peacemaker helped restore order.

Auerbach had told referee Lou Eisenstein to tell Seymour to shut up. Seymour told Eisenstein to tell Auerbach to make him shut up. I think World War I started over less.

After the same game, Cousy stretched himself on a bench with an ice pack on his head. "I felt dizzy and sick to my stomach in the last couple of minutes," he explained. "Three straight—we get them tomorrow!" someone shouted, which prompted Cooz to jump up and stand at attention. He got very patriotic when someone waved an NBA flag.

We handled the Nationals the next day at home, 83–80. We were ready for the St. Louis Hawks with Bob Pettit and the two players the Celtics had traded to get Russell: Cliff Hagan and Ed Macauley. It developed into such a tense series that the Celtics, in a rare display of friction, growled at each other after the Hawks had won the sixth game at home, 96–94, and sent it back to Boston for the final game.

Actually, some players were upset at me because Hagan, my man, had tipped in a missed shot by Pettit as the game ended. "The last thing we said during the time-out," pointed out Ramsey, on the bench when the winning play took place, "was to be sure and block out everyone, but Hagan wasn't blocked."

I was a rookie and felt compelled to defend myself because it had not been my fault. "I was trying to help Loscutoff cover Pettit," I explained. "Pettit got by Loscutoff and I ran over to help out." There was silence and I could understand why because the series meant so much to everyone, and every mistake was that much more serious—that much more magnified. Everything is under a microscope when a championship is involved.

It already had cost Auerbach three hundred dollars for punching owner Ben Kerner before the fourth game in St. Louis. As far as the Celtics were concerned, the three worst places were St. Louis, Syracuse, and Philadelphia, but not necessarily in that order. St. Louis people were mostly agitated by Auerbach, which was something I could not explain, he being such an innocent soul.

Red somehow stimulated emotional frenzy wherever he went. I think he did it deliberately to motivate us. I guess it must have worked, because the Celtics became the best road team for many years. Red triggered the booing, and we played better when we were booed.

St. Louis was on his must-beat list because he dearly loved to irritate Kerner. He had coached for Ben and supposedly they fell out because Kerner had traded some players without Red's knowledge. I think one was Jack Nichols, who later became a Celtic and played for us in the 1957 championship series against the Hawks.

Red said he quit, I heard Kerner fired him. Let's put it this way: Red no longer was in Tri-Cities. There was no doubt bad feelings still existed when the Celtics and Hawks played for the championship some six years later.

We both had fine teams. We won our division and the Hawks won theirs. We had taken a 2–1 lead in the series, and Alex Hannum, the player-coach, I am sure had promised Kerner the Hawks would get even at home in the fourth game.

They did crazy things in those days to psych the other team, such as give the visitors the dirty, old, shiny basketballs while the home team practiced with new ones. Sometimes there wouldn't be enough air in the balls to warm up.

Sharman walked over to the bench while we were shooting around and told Auerbach the basket was low. Sharman was the Bill Bradley of his time. Both could tell the air pressure in a ball by squeezing and the height of the hoop by shooting. They weren't so quick reaching for dinner checks, but that's something else.

"Are you sure?" asked Red, needlessly. "Yeah," said Sharman. "It's about an inch low." Auerbach proceeded to request that the height of the basket be measured, his privilege under the rules.

Kerner came running out from somewhere and accused Red of trying to psych his players and the fans.

One obscene word led to another. Auerbach, being a gentle and subtle individual, punched Kerner right in the mouth before the game even started. That was the basis for the Hawks-Celtics rivalry becoming white hot after it had only been a sizzler. At another game, Red, trying hard to always project an austere image, was hit smack on his bald head by an egg that dripped down his face as he stood there doing the kind of burn Edgar Kennedy made famous in the movies.

Red's dignity was splattered and so was my uniform. "Red," I told him, trying to be funny for a change, "I'm not standing near you anymore." He looked like an omelet.

Kiel Auditorium was a little different than Syracuse, where the fans came out of the stands to escort you to the dressing room as well as frighten the cops away. In Kiel, which was the Metropolitan Opera House of St. Louis, they had people sitting on the stage behind the basket. I think all the unstable fans were put there on purpose. You had to go past them to get to the dressing room, and they were always bumping Auerbach and saying naughty things.

Red, a stickler for defense, always assigned me, Loscutoff, and the next fearsome-looking guy on the club to surround him. When the game started, he had a friend in St. Louis who was a resident FBI agent and he would sit on the bench near Red to protect the rear. There was no evidence that the CIA was involved.

Fun and games. Well, the series went to the seventh game in the Boston Garden with so much riding for the Celtics. If we won, we would earn the magnificent sum of $18,500 in playoff money to split among ourselves. My kids ask me for that to see a movie these days. Compare it with the $20,000 minimum salary that exists in the NBA and you can understand why some athletes moan they were born way ahead of the right time. Now a player on the championship team might get $15,000 for himself.

Money was not the primary object when Russell lined up against Charley Share for the opening tap of the deciding game. You know what Cousy and Sharman were thinking. They were going to win this one if it killed them. They wound up almost killing us.

They wanted the game with a passion, and they chose the final one to play the worst ever. Their shooting was horrible. They were five for forty in their biggest game. They were the real pros. They were supposed to carry the Celtics under pressure but, modestly, a rookie named Heinsohn saved it for them by hitting seventeen of his thirty-three attempts and three foul shots for thirty-seven points.

Cousy had a chance to win it with his second foul shot thirteen seconds from the end of regulation but missed, and Pettit hit two free throws to tie at 103–103. Sharman had a chance to win it six seconds later but hit the front rim with a jumper he always made. It was that kind of night for both of them.

Sharman had another opportunity to win it in the first overtime but missed a twenty-five-footer at the buzzer. I guess Russell and me, the rookies, were the only ones not emotionally exhausted as we regrouped on the sidelines for the second overtime. I was excited as well as convinced I had better keep shooting if we were to survive.

I was living dangerously in foul trouble but I could not afford to worry about that because Sharman and Cousy were so nervous. I had to keep going bang, bang, bang everytime they gave me the ball. Everything worked, even my passing. I had all those people in the Boston Garden screaming for me with Cousy and Sharman on the floor.

I was the one everyone now was depending on to bring that first championship to Boston. It was a flattering position for a rookie, and I am sure I would have been excused if my line drives had suddenly stopped going in for the next five minutes.

I always liked the big challenge. I always seemed to respond best when a shot had to be made or a rebound had to be tipped in. Maybe that's what Auerbach saw in me when he was telling the outside world my attitude was bad, I didn't hustle, and I wouldn't be able to handle the contact in the NBA.

I only lasted three minutes in the second overtime but I hit three shots and grabbed two rebounds. I hit a twenty-foot jumper to put us ahead, 121–120, and then they called the sixth foul on me. Naturally, I made a scene. I didn't want to leave with so much at stake. It was like a kid being sent to bed just when the party was about to start. They had to push and lead me away.

I was so overwrought, I began heading for the dressing room. Someone reminded me the game wasn't over, so I had to go to the bench and cry in front of all those people. All the emotion that I thought was safely dammed inside burst as the Celtics crowded around Auerbach near midcourt to hear him complain about the foul against me.

I threw my warmup jacket over my head and brought the sleeve up to my eyes to hide the tears. That's what they mean when they say basketball, football, and baseball are games of emotion. Big, strong, physical beings who have fearlessly faced the Wilt Chamberlains, Bob Laniers, and Wayne Embrys have been known to cry like your kid brother.

I sat alone as the argument continued, with Red losing another one. Then the others joined me on the bench for the remaining two minutes that were to become agonizingly long. It was as though Cousy, Sharman, and Auerbach were destined to endure the strain of anticipation as long as possible.

I couldn't believe that two minutes could be so long in a sport where time keeps moving. So much happened in such little time after I left the game. The Hawks tied it, and Ramsey made a foul and basket to put us ahead by three points.

That should have been the end, but St. Louis was within a point, 124–123, with twenty-seven seconds to go and had the ball. Alex Hannum, the player-coach, had just put himself into the playoffs for the first time because three of his big men had fouled out, and he lost possession for walking while trying to set up Pettit.

I was peeking from under my jacket by then. We had eight seconds to kill, and Loscutoff made a foul for a two-point lead with one second to go. Over, now? Not yet. Hannum took the ball out and flung it all the way to the other end off the backboard. The ball bounced to the foul line, where Pettit actually got a shot off before the buzzer.

To make a short story a little longer, the ball skidded off the rim and Share almost put in the rebound. It no doubt would not have counted, but the Celtics did not stand around and wonder. We were off our feet and into the clouds. People came pouring onto the floor and engulfed us. Loscutoff and Russell raised Auerbach to their shoulders before he could light his cigar and carried him through the mob.

Our dressing room looked like Shea Stadium the day they tore up the place after the Mets won the World Series. "Heinsohn! Heinsohn! Heinsohn!" was all I heard. That was the pleasure of the thing. We really were a great team. The togetherness. Those Celtics wanted to win it so badly, and I had played well, and we had won it.

I respected Cousy, Sharman, and the other fellows so much, it made me feel that much better I had done so much to help them win. I sneaked away to the table in the trainer's room because I didn't want to get trampled in the dressing room. I grabbed a beer and had the trainer look at the knee I had skinned when someone dropped me after a shoulder ride on the court.

Red lit his first championship cigar and was thrown into his first championship shower. I walked over to Russell and held his head while Auerbach shaved off the beard—which was promised if we went all the way. "At least," said Russ, "I've still got my mustache."

A championship dressing room is for little boys, not grown men. Everyone got sprayed with beer because the Celtics had not acquired champagne taste at that early stage of their championship development. Guys put their arms around each other and said innocuous things that made them laugh, anyway. Silly but nothing like it.

Auerbach said the serious things for himself, Cousy, and Sharman. "We have been chasing this for seven years," announced Red, beer and water from the shower dripping on his drenched cigar. "My nervous system is shot. What can you say?"

Can you imagine Auerbach at a loss for words? That's what the 1957 championship meant to everyone, especially me. I was too tired to speak about me, so I let Sharman tell the world what I had just contributed to the history of sports.

"I never saw a rookie play like that," Bill told the writers. "Greatest pressure game ever. What a show he put on. Hey, Tom, give me five, boy. You and Russell. You're not rookies anymore."

Oh, yes. Bill Russell.

6

"HEY, BILL," I said to Russell alongside me. "Give me an autograph for my kid cousin, will you?" We were sitting in Madison Square Garden watching part of a doubleheader not long after Russ had returned from the 1956 Olympics to join the Celtics in mid-December.

I was the rookie, having been with the team since the start of the season, and he was the rookie rookie. As the veteran of the combination, I never expected to hear what I heard. "No," he said.

He had to be kidding. Cousy and Sharman were sitting in the same row, and I had just gotten their autographs. "Russ," I persisted, "this is my cousin. This is my real cousin."

I figured that would reach him. He had been with the team only a few weeks and already had given indications as to how he felt about autographs. So he didn't sign when he came out of the locker room. I was his teammate—he'd sign for me. He should, anyway.

"Look," he said, "I'm not going to sign." I badgered him because I still couldn't believe he wouldn't put his name on a piece of paper for me. "If I sign for him," he explained, "I've got to sign for everybody, and I want to watch the game."

So I let him watch the game and never bothered him again as long as we were teammates. He never knew that I was the one who forged his name on team basketballs throughout the years. That was the least I could do for someone who did so much to protect me and all the other Celtics on defense. We were even—he covered for me on defense, and I covered for him on autographed balls.

Russell the player was obvious. Russell the person was an enigma. He was tough to live with, which was understandable once I got to understand him a little. Nobody understood Russell entirely— including himself at times. He was the first black I had ever played with and with whom I was to have such close contact. In addition, he was no ordinary black. He was Bill Russell, six-ten, the best college basketball player among some outstanding college players in the country, including me. He was Bill Russell, a man with demanding pride and a deep hurt that drove him onward and upward in his search for answers.

Our paths had crossed only once in college ball and, I guess, that game sort of established the early relationship between us. We did play in the East-West game in Kansas City, but it was an All-Star thing that meant nothing. The Holiday Festival in Madison Square at Christmas in 1955 had real significance.

Everyone made our semifinal Festival game a personal challenge. It was Russell vs. Heinsohn. Russ and K. C. Jones had led the San Francisco Dons to a thirty-four-game winning streak that reached back to December 4, 1954. They were seeded first, and UCLA with Willie Naulls was seeded second.

Russell had the reputation on the West Coast, while my shooting and rebounding had impressed people on the East Coast. So the pregame talk and strategy centered on us. Roy Leening, our coach at Holy Cross, tried to tempt Phil Woolpert, the Dons' coach, to play Russell on me.

Leening said I would be playing Russ, but he didn't think San Francisco had the nerve to put Russell on me defensively. Woolpert agreed, indicating he was a smart coach. There were such headlines as: "Heinsohn Will Cover Russell Tonight but Russell Won't Cover Heinsohn" and "Heinsohn to Pit Skill Against Russell."

The next day's paper carried this enlightening headline: "Heinsohn, Holy Cross No Match for Dons' Bill Russell." That was correct. I managed only twelve points while Russell, not necessarily an offensive player, contributed twenty-four to his team's 67–51 victory. I became a fan of Russell the player right then. I roughed him up on defense but that only made him more determined.

I gave out this analysis after the game: "That Russell has great reflexes. We found him pretty easy to box out, but you can't stop him within three feet of the basket. He can't hit from outside, though.

"I figure I did a better job on him than I did on Bob Pettit in the Sugar Bowl two years ago, but it wasn't enough. Pettit, of course, was a better all-around player." I don't know if Russ read that but, if he did, he probably didn't like the idea that I felt Pettit had been tougher for me.

Russell was like that. He had an ego bigger than himself or mine or Cousy's or any of the Celtics. He was proud of his accomplishments and had every right, but what annoyed him was that few people gave him the proper recognition.

He felt that the way he rebounded, played defense, and blocked shots for a championship college team made it obvious he was an unusual player. Yet, on the West Coast, for example, they once picked Kenny Sears of Santa Clara over him as Player of the Year. He never forgave Sears or the people responsible for such a ridiculous thing.

Russell rationalized it as a typical black-white attitude. I wouldn't accept such a racial explanation in those days, but through my years with the Celtics after Russell joined the team I learned there were such things. I was brought up in white neighborhoods and was never exposed to black experiences until I began playing and traveling with Russell, K. C. Jones, Sam Jones, and Satch Sanders. Then I was reminded of the Italian and Irish kids beating up the German kid, and we all had white skin.

I knew only Russell the player because of the Holiday Festival and relayed my knowledge of him to Walter Brown and Red Auerbach. I told them of what I had learned from that game. The day of my press conference, the media asked how I felt about Russell.

I proceeded to tell them what a great player Russell was going to be. I told them how I faked and drove by him a good five feet and he still blocked my shot. He had done it two or three times and that had been proof enough for me.

He had such remarkable reflexes and recovery. I could see the potential. You just couldn't outrebound him. He reached out and recovered rebounds that were ten feet away. Red and Walter Brown seemed most anxious to be reassured by that. The Celtics had the speed and the scoring but the missing dimension was someone who could get the ball and play defense. I was Russell's private publicity man.

I believe I convinced them that Russell would have a defensive impact on the NBA. On the basis of what I said to Red and Walter Brown, they had me devote half my own press conference to explaining what I knew about Russell. I became part of the selling job.

I did not realize that Russell was going to be Auerbach's pet project. Red, knowing Boston as well as people, was aware that it was not going to be easy selling Russ as a player or person. He had conducted a complete study of Russell and discovered he was complicated enough in every respect for the average mind to find him difficult to comprehend.

Auerbach was thorough about such things. He never has been influenced by the statistics of a player, no matter how impressive. He was the one who established the Celtic prototype and always has been most demanding and selective in that respect. He talked to many people about Russell, including his coach, to determine his substantive qualities and then made the decision to trade Ed Macauley and Cliff Hagan because he was convinced Russell met his standards.

Red believed in Russell from the beginning, though he recognized that his attributes were novel to basketball at that time. Auerbach has been successful in pro basketball because he has had the insight and vision that enabled him to pick the right talent and then mold the different personalities into his kind of team. Pro basketball in those days was a run and shoot game, but Red recognized that Russell could revolutionize everything with his rebounding, defense, and shot-blocking.

Russell represented a new force in pro basketball that the people in the Boston area could in no way understand at that stage. New England was hockey, track, and Red Sox territory until it became Cousy country. The Cousy excitement concentrated on him, not pro basketball. Cooz came along and could do no wrong, something the newspapermen reminded Auerbach of anytime he lost his perspective.

I cite as an example of the Cousy mystique something that was told to me about Al McGuire, the Marquette coach. Allie was a substitute on the Knicks from 1951 to 1954. His brother Dick normally played Cousy in one of the better confrontations of those days. My wife, Diane, the basketball player, still considers the McGuire-Cousy matchup she watched on television when she was a New Jersey schoolgirl one of the most stimulating of all time.

Allie would get to relieve brother Dick for a few minutes whenever coach Joe Lapchick considered it strategically wise. It was on one of those occasions in Boston that Allie, quick with words, hopped onto the trainer's table after the game and announced to the world: "I own Bob Cousy."

He was kidding, of course. He had replaced his brother for only a few minutes and had contributed nothing of substance. But he had seen Clif Keane, the supreme Cousy worshiper among the worshiping Boston press, walking into the dressing room and couldn't resist the temptation of needling him. Allie had no idea of the magic of his statement until the Knicks reappeared in Boston and the Garden sold out then and regularly, thereafter, whenever Lapchick's team came to town.

Al McGuire had insulted Cousy, the American flag of Boston, and the superpatriots were angry enough to buy more tickets than the box office usually sold. "That remark," acknowledged Allie, a marginal player, "kept me in the league at least two more years." That was the nature of Cousy's strength in Boston, and Auerbach knew that represented a serious problem trying to sell Russell, a strange one, to that public.

I was considered a fine basketball player when I signed with the Celtics but not in the class of Russell. He was ahead of his time when he came to pro basketball. No one was ready for him. Auerbach was cast in the role of John the Baptist. He had to walk before Russell and spread the gospel to those who considered Cousy a religion unto himself.

It was not an easy job in many respects. Red had to establish mutual respect with Russell, naturally apprehensive and supersensitive about racial relationships, and then sell his strange game and stranger social attitudes to the Cousy cult. Red never gave Russell special treatment within the scope of the Celtic operations but did go out of his way to merchandise the man.

I assume Russ recognized that and the sincerity of Auerbach's desire to make him feel comfortable in an uncomfortable situation. Chuck Cooper had been the first black to play NBA basketball in Boston, and he had retired at the end of the 1955–56 season. Chuck and Don Barksdale, who had played two seasons with the Celtics, had made absolutely no dent on the racial attitudes of the people, and now there was Russell, bigger, better, and more menacing.

I am talking, of course, from hindsight. I must admit, at first I was not that aware (and cared less) of the problems Russell would confront or would create for whatever reasons, justified or unjustified. My interest in Russell was pure, simple, and selfish: He had the ability to make the Celtics the best pro basketball team in the NBA.

I sure learned a lot about Russell, myself, and the more important aspects of man's relationships with man—whatever the size, shape, or color. Russ came to the team a very guarded individual. As I look back at it, what he did through the years was not understood by many people. He was an independent soul and apparently felt he was not obligated to explain himself to those mentalities that had been indifferent and insulting to Russell the black person before and after he became Russell the famous basketball player.

He once tried explaining in a magazine article for *Sports Illustrated* and people still did not understand. He mentioned how difficult it was to trust white people because of bad experiences he enumerated, and the conclusion was that he hated all whites. He said he owed nothing to the fans, so the people and some members of the media became even angrier at him than they had been for other things that bothered them.

Truthfully, there was no practical reason why people had to be put in the position of understanding Russell. If he was trying to reach the bigots, of which there are many in this country, he was wasting his time. If he was trying to embarrass those who were not prejudiced but were submissive or not aggressive for whatever reason, he was adding to their confusion about him.

Russell did have justifiable reasons for being angry and impatient with the oppressive and prejudicial attitudes he confronted. I, as a white teammate, was embarrassed, enraged, and sometimes confused by what I should do about the treatment Russell, Sam and K. C. Jones, and Satch Sanders were forced to face in the normal pursuit of playing ball and entertaining the very people who insulted them because they happened to be born a different color.

Russell never really sat with me and itemized the things that disturbed him. I learned the hard way—when we went on the road and he wasn't allowed to eat in certain restaurants with us. I learned even more about him when I heard some of the childhood incidents that had left indelible scars on his memory.

How his twelve-year-old brother Charlie was arrested for shining shoes on a Louisiana street reserved for white shoeshine boys. How his father, after Bill's mother died in Oakland, went back to fish in Monroe, Louisiana, with an old white friend, who said: "Yeah, Charlie, you always were a good nigger." How the family left the bigotry of the South to move to California and he vowed to fight the twisted world he had left behind to his dying breath.

Those things are impossible to forget when they happen to you. There were things that were impossible for me to forget that didn't even happen to me. For example, my first experience with the bigotry that confronted Russell soon after he joined the Celtics, and made him resent being treated as a first-class player but a second-class citizen.

In 1956, our rookie year, we were in St. Louis, one of the major antiblack cities in the league as well as the country at the time. The Knicks, for example, could not get accommodations at the top hotels because they had Ray Felix and Sweetwater Clifton, so they had to stay at the Mark Twain. The Hotel Jefferson eventually yielded, and I believe it was Jackie Robinson and the Brooklyn Dodgers who broke down the Chase Hotel, one of the elite white establishments.

I was put in a room at the Melbourne Hotel in St. Louis with Russell because Jack Nichols, his regular roomie, was attending dental classes and could not travel. After the game, I suggested to Russ that we go across the street from the hotel and have something to eat in a greasy spoon that was open late. He declined. I asked why and he explained he had tried to eat there but they wouldn't serve him because he was black.

I had never thought about that because I never had that problem. I had taken it for granted that everyone was entitled to at least eat whenever and wherever he desired. That's when I really started looking at Bill Russell the person. My attitude toward him changed immediately.

I was a little annoyed about his not signing autographs but I suddenly realized he had some cross to bear. I told Cousy about the restaurant incident and he recalled some of Chuck Cooper's experiences when they were roommates.

That was the beginning of my education on the times and bad times of Bill Russell, black basketball player. A few years later, after K. C. Jones, Sam Jones, and Satch Sanders had joined us, we went South to play some exhibition games, and I was given an advanced course.

I think it was in Charlotte, North Carolina, that they made the black players stay in a black hotel. Walter Brown had promised Russell he never would be placed in such a humiliating position, but there had been a mixup in communications or something. Russell and the others played the game under the circumstances, but Russ talked to Red and Walter Brown and was assured it never would happen again. There was more to come.

A couple of years later, in the 1961–62 season, we went to Marion, Indiana, for an exhibition game. Marion was about 100 to 150 miles from Chicago and considered a northern city. At least, I would consider it northern coming from New Jersey.

We got to the town and they gave us a fabulous reception with banquet attached. The mayor was there to greet us, and many of the fifty thousand residents had taken time to cheer the champions of the NBA. We were all pleased by the warm, sincere display of hospitality. Everyone was given a key to the city—a wooden one, painted gold with "welcome" inscribed on it.

Under those circumstances, we assumed we were welcome. I have since learned what many have tried to teach me in many ways: Do not assume anything. "Oh, gee, my first key to the city," said some of the guys. Some were kidding, some were serious.

We played the game at a high school and then went to the hotel, dropped off our bags, and headed for the only eating place open. It was sort of a club or cafe. Not the most elegant place. Frankly, it was a one-armed joint with a juke box.

I think I was with Cousy, Sharman, and Ramsey. We got there

first and the others wandered over in groups. We were just finishing our food when Russell walked in with Carl Braun and K. C. Jones. The guy at the bar wouldn't let them eat. Right place, wrong color for Russ and K.C.

We noticed the conversation but didn't know what it was about. Russell and K.C. left, and Braun came to our table ripping mad. "Some damn place this is," he shouted. "Marion, Indiana. They give us a banquet, the keys to the city. Everything's beautiful but they won't let Russ and K.C. eat here because they're black."

Carl began looking around as though he were going to remodel the place. "Let's find out where the mayor lives," he suggested, "and give him back his goddamn keys. I'm going to tell him to shove it." It was around 12:30 A.M., and our only regret was that it wasn't three or four in the morning once we agreed with Carl.

We filled two cabs with black and white players. Braun was the leader because it had been his idea, so he knocked on the door. The mayor opened it and we obviously had awakened him. That was good.

"Mayor, I'm Carl Braun from the Boston Celtics," said Carl. "I am here with some of my teammates, and we would like you to take the keys you gave us today and shove them. . . ." Unfortunately, the mayor was not about to be that accommodating. He did express his regret, which meant nothing to Russell, who already led the league in regrets.

Our next game was in Lexington, Kentucky, and our black players ran into northern hospitality, southern style, right on top of Marion, Indiana. Before I recall what happened, I think this is the time to say that for the nine years I played with the Celtics, there was only one instance where a player yelled at another player. Just one incident in all those years, and it was an innocent mistake that could have become a serious problem if Auerbach had not nipped it and we didn't have people who took time to understand.

It was before a playoff game in St. Louis, where the dressing rooms in Kiel Auditorium were built for show business, not sports. They were small with big mirrors and an edging of light bulbs for entertainers to make up. Gene Guarilia was getting dressed in one with Sam Jones.

Guarilia, a fine player but a reserve on the ball club, got involved in a conversation with Sam and inadvertently said "Sambo." I am sure it was Gene's way of trying to be friendly, not insulting, and he meant it strictly as an innocent extension of Sam.

Sam, normally a calm, pleasant individual, must have been nervous about the game because he exploded. He actually got angry enough to punch Guarilia out if Red and the guys on the team had not cooled it. Sam accepted the explanation that no racial slur had been intended, and it was forgotten. All the racial tensions came from outside sources.

Yet I am sure Russell had to wonder about the degree and sincerity of our concern in view of what took place in Lexington. The game was to be in honor of Ramsey and Hagan, who had played as Kentucky teammates in that very fieldhouse. Their children were to be given scholarships in a pregame ceremony.

It was to be the first game at the university with integrated seating. Blacks always had been restricted to certain sections, but this time they would be permitted to sit anyplace. In view of what had just happened in Marion, Auerbach reassured Russell, Sam Jones, K. C. Jones, and Sanders that everything was set in Lexington. There would be no racial issues at the hotel. Everyone could eat and sleep as equal American citizens.

Russell was informed that everything had been discussed with the hotel people and no one would be embarrassed. Both teams checked in. The St. Louis Hawks also had black players and there was no trouble registering.

It was about noon, so I went to my room with the luggage and then headed for the coffee shop. I was eating with a couple of the guys when Sanders and Sam Jones showed up and the waitress refused to let them in. Oh, no. Not again?

Yes, again. I was then told by Buddy Leroux, our trainer, that the black players had held a meeting and decided to go home. They weren't going to play. First Marion and now Lexington. Could you blame them?

I know how I felt when I saw the look on Sanders' face. He was crushed. Satch was from New York City and never had experienced such treatment there. I never had more compassion for anyone than I had for him at that moment. I respected him with a passion and considered him one of the finest human beings I've ever known.

The situation put me and the other players in an awkward position. Auerbach tried to get Russell to consider playing because the game was for Ramsey, his teammate, and the desegregating of seats represented a step forward. "There's no way . . . you promised us . . ." said Russell, "and we're leaving."

He was right but now what do the other players do? Red came to the lobby to tell us the black players were going home. He said he had explained to Russell it obviously had been done by a bigoted waitress on her own, since the hotel had cleared everything. Russ took Sam Jones, K. C. Jones, and Sanders to the airport with him, anyway.

"What's gonna happen now?" I asked Red. "We're gonna play the game," he said. "We have a contract to play it." I have to admit that was a helluva spot to be in. Here I was in complete sympathy with Russell and the others. We had played, traveled, and fought together. Should we walk together?

Russell never said a word to us. He left us to the dictates of our consciences. We had only six players left because we went to Lexington with only ten men. We talked about it. We considered telling Lexington to screw it.

I am sure from the viewpoint of Russell, Sam, K.C., and Satch that there never should have been a struggle within ourselves. They placed no demands on us, but I am certain they would have felt a lot better about our sense of values if we had left with them.

I can truthfully say we played because of Ramsey and that's all. I can truthfully say I was not sure I was doing the right thing. In my mind, I thought of how Russell might interpret our decision to stay because of his experiences with attitudes and responses. When it was time for his white teammates to stand up, they never were counted until they went to the game and six uniforms were handed out.

My answer to that as I look back is that sometimes there are no simple answers. One man's simplistic solution might be another man's complication. There were influences on both sides, and Russell was intelligent or discreet enough not to make it an issue. I prefer to think he knew his teammates were not prejudiced and the Lexington decision simply was a matter of judgment—good, poor, or bad.

Playing with Russell constantly put you in a position of explaining what he was like. As the people began recognizing his impact on the world of pro basketball, his lifestyle became more prominent. His personality generated a charisma that added to his mystique.

It got to be similar to what is Johnny Carson really like or

Muhammad Ali or even Tommy Heinsohn? Russell was a mystery, and I guess it always will be that way. Only he knew himself, and he preferred to let the curious dangle.

I think we saw that in the way he handled the invitation to his induction into the Hall of Fame. As I understand it, he indicated he would attend and then said he would not. I got the impression he sat out there in Seattle and cackled over the disturbance he triggered. I believe he enjoyed the sight of those who never cared to take the time to understand what he had said about racial attitudes in the *SI* magazine article and elaborated on in his book now saying: "I don't understand that guy."

Russell never was one for ceremonies. He apparently put such things in the same category as signing autographs. He had learned what the key to the city of Marion, Indiana, meant, for example. He had learned what the people of Boston really thought deep inside when he tried to move to a better house in the same neighborhood.

I don't think Russell ever talks about that incident, but it was the first and only time I saw him cry. One year after we had won the championship, he moved to the town of Reading, outside of Boston. He had trouble finding a home there at first, but repeated championships opened the door for him.

Ultimately, he became such a popular resident because of the Celtic excitement, they held a huge party for him at the country club. We all went—the whole team. He got up to talk and I'd never seen him more moved. He really could put words together, seriously or otherwise. The world eventually learned about his erudition and wry humor when he worked on the ABC-TV game of the week.

For example, Dave DeBusschere and Jerry Lucas constantly created confusion when they played for the Knicks because people thought they looked alike. Russell was asked if he noticed the resemblance. "Don't ask me," he answered. "They all look alike to me." He could say things as though some professional wrote them for him.

This particular day he really was touched. He made the statement that he considered Reading his home, and he began crying. He told the people he never wanted to leave there. All he wanted, as it later developed, was to buy a better home in the same area because *he* could afford it.

He wanted a bigger and nicer house for Rose and the kids.

What did those wonderful people of Reading with higher priced homes do? They began circulating a petition about a black trying to move near them. Another example of the things that drove Russell deeper into a shell. In his position, whom could he really trust?

He found it difficult to believe that the fans, media, or anyone actually gave a damn about Russell the person. I believe that is why he refused to be part of the special ceremony for the retiring of his Celtic number. Auerbach did the next best thing by having him introduced when Russell came to Boston for a TV assignment. It was Red's way of telling the fans that the No. 6 would hang from the ceiling of the Boston Garden with the numbers of other Celtic greats —including the No. 1 for Walter Brown.

How did Russell acknowledge the crowd reaction? He never got off his seat. He just sat at the announcers' table at midcourt and felt uncomfortable, if anything. He wasn't about to compromise his principles for applause.

I actually had compassion for Russell though we were so different and competitive at times. He was an issues person, I was a people person. He judged people on issues, I judged them as people. To each his own. He liked people, but I guess he wouldn't come to grips with too many because of his background. He had been hurt too much.

He never let anyone get too close to him, which is why his friendship with Ronnie Watts seemed strange to me and even Auerbach, who knew them both better than I did. Ronnie turned out to be the friend Russell called on the Bell Telephone television commercials. That was no put-on. They are close friends to this day.

I assume it developed while Watts was with the Celtics for two seasons. He was a forward out of Wake Forest and played only one game in 1965–66 and twenty-seven when Russell became coach the next season. It was hard to explain why Watts and not K. C. Jones or John Havlicek or even Tommy Heinsohn.

They continued their friendship after Watts left the team and Russell went to Washington, which was Ron's hometown, to tape a television series with Senator Ted Kennedy, Governor Wallace, and others. Russell obviously felt comfortable with Ronnie to the extent they frequently talked long distance when Russ moved to Seattle. I don't think the telephone company gave them free privileges as part of their television deal, either. I repeat, Russell could be complicated, and I think after a while he enjoyed the idea of complicating things and confusing people.

There were those always trying to complicate things for him. One day after I had quit playing, I heard some sportswriters saying they were going to get him. He had just become coach of the Celtics with the help, I believe, of a recommendation from me. The writers were annoyed because Russell would not co-operate. They mentioned the autograph business, how he refused to communicate with the press, and everything they did not like about him and his attitude.

I was well aware of how the Boston press and other newspapermen around the country felt about him. On a popularity scale from one to ten, he would have owed points. He had the same low opinion of them. He had come to Boston and been given rough treatment and, consequently, extended them the same courtesy.

Being quite perceptive, he judged people by what kind of sandpaper they were—in other words, how abrasive they would be to him. He learned that when he was a kid, and he told me about some of the influences, eventually.

For those who wonder what players discuss in a shower, one day we were discussing the investment Russell was making in a rubber plantation in Liberia. My reaction was he was either a genius or the most stupid man in the world for investing his dough in a rubber plantation in Africa. From there we went into his background and how he was in the police lineup all the time as a kid because the Louisiana police would round up black kids as routine procedure. That was why he grew up sensitive to racial prejudices and, until he matured later in Boston, was wary of the press, because of its awesome power and the questionable attitudes of some writers.

He was always concerned about the press promoting a white player over a black. He made statements about the quota system in the NBA that placed an unwritten limit on black players on each team, partly to see if he could stimulate the press to use its influence about it. The Kenny Sears situation was black and white to him. Maybe it was, maybe it wasn't, but Russ was sure Sears had been pushed by the media and most people over him because of color.

I think he was right because there were prejudiced sportswriters in Boston and all over the country. He wasn't always right, especially when he did and said things to me that easily could have turned me off—for example, the night I received notice from the league office that I had just been named Rookie of the Year.

7

We Were Sitting in the dressing room in the Boston Garden, getting ready for a playoff game with the Syracuse Nationals in my rookie season. On my right was Russell, on my left Cousy, which was as it should have been.

I was between greatness and two super egos. The interesting part of the Celtics in those days was how Auerbach managed to get the most out of those two without being destroyed. They were both basketball geniuses, which is why I felt good sitting between them. Something might rub off.

It was standard procedure, even then, for me to get notices from the NBA about my technicals. I went through my mail and found a letter from the league office. Russell looked over and began cackling like only he can cackle.

"Whatcha do, get another fine?" he asked. "Well, it looks like it," I replied. I opened the envelope and a check dropped out. Could it be a refund? I looked at the check and it was for three hundred dollars.

I read the letter with Russell looking over my shoulder. It said: "We are happy to inform you that you have been selected Rookie of the Year, and you will find your prize money that is attached to that award." Russell looked at me and I grinned at him.

I picked up the check and got off my stool. "I think you ought to give me half of that," he said. "What do you mean?" I asked. "Well," he said, "if I'd been here the whole season, you never would've gotten it." I said: "Oh, is that right?" An eloquent exchange, right? The sonofagun actually meant it.

I sat there and said to myself: "Now, isn't that something. Imagine him saying that—and in the playoffs, no less?" He had a way of getting under your skin when least expected. Once in a while he would take shots at me in the paper. Why, I don't know, unless he was trying to be candid at my expense.

One of his most precious statements bothers me to this day. Someone asked about me at a press conference and he said: "What they ought to do with Heinsohn is run him until he drops and throw a bucket of water over him and run him more." I was supposed to be out of shape, and that was why I couldn't play forty-eight minutes.

Auerbach had made similar remarks before he drafted me. I was too fat for him or something like that. Cousy also had a few bright things to contribute on the subject. When Auerbach, Russell, and Cousy all said it, then it had to be, so everyone believed it. What none of them cared to consider was my viewpoint. They were thoughtful that way.

I had good reason why I couldn't play forty-eight minutes. From my high school days, I always was an intense, emotional player. I never really learned to pace myself because I couldn't the way I played. Cousy, of course, had the ball all the time and he slowed it down whenever he wanted. Russell was famous for not coming down on offense a lot, which enabled him to be back on defense if necessary and, also, rest awhile.

Auerbach didn't have to worry about working forty-eight minutes because he sat on his job most of the time—though, I must admit, he was in motion more than any other coach when fast-breaking the referees. I was the big slob. I was the one they picked on, which was fine because I was afraid to imagine what would have happened to that wonderful team concept of ours if Cousy had said something nasty about Russell and vice versa.

In all honesty the amazing thing about the Celtics was the team pride Auerbach developed. I don't know how he did it because Red could be harsh and abrasive in his own way, but General MacArthur didn't create more determination and togetherness when he promised that he and his troops would return. I think the Celtics respected Auerbach because he was the Celtics and they sincerely believed he knew what he was doing.

Except, of course, when he was driving. Red was Evel Knievel before his time. If Red could have jumped a car over the Grand Canyon he would have done it without thinking—which was the way he drove. His reputation preceded him to the point where everyone suggested he had another ride whenever Red extended an invitation.

Gene Conley made the mistake of joining the coach one time when we were on an exhibition tour before the season. Generally, the rookies were the only ones who would ride with Red because they were in no position to turn him down. We all knew when we were going to exhibition games, never to get into a car with Auerbach.

We probably should have had the right of refusal written into our contracts, but we never thought of it. The Players' Association was not that strong in those days, anyway. Conley had been away for five years working his pitching skills and had absolutely no power position when he returned to the Celtics in 1958–59.

We headed for Maine for our first exhibition game. If you've ever gone up the Maine Turnpike in October, you know how foggy it can get. The fog rolled in from the ocean and blanketed the meadows and the road. There was nothing a normal person could do but be extremely cautious.

Red, not being a normal person behind the wheel, was not bothered by such conservative practices as driving carefully. He proceeded to go eighty-five miles an hour through the velvet curtain. Conley froze in his seat. "The man's crazy," he said to the only person in the car to whom he had the courage to say it—himself.

It was as though Red was trying to qualify at Indianapolis. His only guide was the white divider in the middle of the road, and he followed it without deviation. In his mind, the line represented radar and, therefore, he was not driving blind.

Conley was. He was afraid to open his eyes. Once in a while he peeked out of fear but saw nothing. He even found it tough seeing the white line that Red was using as a steering beam.

There was one thing Gene managed to see for a fleeting moment. A Howard Johnson building zipped by extremely close on his side. Auerbauch never blinked. He was following the white line and never noticed he had just driven through Howard Johnson's parking lot and out the other side.

That was the fun side of Auerbach. Underneath that heart of cold was a man who enjoyed a laugh or two or three, as long as it wasn't on him. I'll never forget the time we had an apple war.

Come on. You never heard of an apple war? Through a lapse of memory or at the point of a gun, I was driving with Auerbach that day. It was another of our trips through the countryside on the way to an exhibition game.

Whenever we had time to waste, we would play an intellectual game called "Zit." It worked this way: If you saw a cemetery and identified it first, you got a point. If you were first to see a dog, you got a point. Anytime you saw a dog lifting his leg, you got five points. Anytime you saw two dogs making love, you hit the jackpot. You would have to yell "cemetery" or "dog," and you automatically won the game.

Forget that we all were supposed to be college graduates—it was better than playing ghost or word games. It was an ideal time-consumer for the two-hundred-mile drive to Pittsfield, Massachusetts. We called time to buy a bushel of apples that we split with Cousy and the other guys.

We resumed playing Zit, at high stakes—lunch to the winner. We were having a great time driving through the mountains, taking bites of apples and tossing them out the window. Such luxury.

Suddenly, Cousy pulled from behind us, drove his car alongside, and there was a broadside of apples. It became a war on the highway —like pirate ships side by side firing at each other. It was Auerbach's car against Cousy's car and some battle.

Red was weaving all over the white line and Cooz was hugging the inside. Some guys took bites and heaved the apples like hand grenades with proper sound effects. Everyone was laughing and screaming and then we heard a different but familiar sound: "Rrrrrrr!"

It sounded like a cop's car. It was a cop's car. The cop pulled alongside Red's car and motioned him over, but Cousy kept going, the master of the fast break as usual.

"What the hell do you guys think you're doing?" said the cop.

"Well," said Red, innocently, "we were playing Zit." Auerbach had to find the one cop along the highway to Pittsfield, Massachusetts, who had never played Zit. The cop never even heard of it.

Red changed directions on him. "Officer," said Red, turning on the charm, "I'm sorry. I'm Red Auerbach, coach of the Boston Celtics. I know I'm wrong." The cop wasn't impressed at all. He invited Red to follow him to the home of the justice of the peace.

We had to drive up the mountain, through back roads, to get to the man's house. He was the judge, of course, and the cop explained that Red had been speeding over the white line and acting as though he had been drinking. "They were throwing apples," added the cop.

"Throwing apples?" said the judge as though he might have had a case for the resident psychiatrist. "We were having an apple war," elaborated Red, figuring the judge would understand that. He didn't, so Red had to backtrack and explain that we had been playing Zit and what that was, and we were driving along just having fun and killing time, which accounted for the apple war.

At that point, Mr. Auerbach was not my candidate for defense counsel. I figured we would all wind up killing time in a dirty jail. Certainly, Red deserved it, but he somehow escaped only to make it another time at another place.

On that occasion, we were in Cincinnati for a regular-season game and had just won a close one. We were heading for the dressing room when there was a commotion. A rather large one, to be accurate. We kept right on going, the safest thing when the bad guys are in the wrong corral. Auerbach came in after we reached the locker room and yelled: "That guy better not do that again!"

What happened, Red? "That guy took a swing at me," he said. "He kicked me. I took a swing at him. I knocked his glasses off and knocked him right on his can. He can't do that to me. I took care of him, okay." We were impressed.

We went back to the hotel and two policemen showed up in the lobby. "Where's Red Auerbach?" "I don't know where he is," they were told. Just then Red walked out of the elevator.

"Are you Red Auerbach," the cops asked, nicely. "Yes," he said modestly. "You're under arrest," they said, not so modestly. "For what?" asked Red, shaken. "Assault and battery," said the cops. "The guy hit me," said Red, scared. "I never hit the guy." All of a sudden he was a devout pacifist.

Nevertheless, they took him to jail and locked him up. Cousy and Buddy Leroux went with him for moral support and came back to the hotel without him. "We need three hundred dollars to bail him out," announced Cousy. "He hasn't any money on him. If we don't raise the money, he has to stay in jail."

Some considered that the best offer we might get. "Don't bail him out," I suggested. "Yeah," said Cousy, recognizing the practicality of the rare opportunity to get Auerbach. "Let's leave him overnight. He's got no television. He can't send out for Chinese food. He's got no cigars. It'll kill him."

We decided that valor was not the best part of a practical joke at Red's expense under prison conditions. "I've only got twenty-five dollars," I said, opening the bids. We raised the three hundred dollars somehow and finally got Red out of jail around three in the morning.

Red got in touch with me after breakfast. "You're gonna have to testify," he said. "Testify to what?" I asked. "You've got to testify that this guy kicked me," he said. He was frightened and I loved it. "I didn't see the guy kick you, Red," I told him, innocently. "I wasn't even there when it happened."

He glared at me. It never was difficult to know when Red was getting mad. "You saw the guy kick me," he said, almost shouting while emphasizing "you" and "kick." He was tampering with a witness, but I was sure he, at least, would never squeal.

"I did see the guy kick you?" I asked. "Didn't you see the guy kick me?" he asked, daring me to deny it once more. "Yeah, I saw the guy kick you," I agreed, delivering the proper message.

He nodded. To make sure, our little godfather said: "If *you* don't want to wind up in Minneapolis, *you* saw the guy kick me." I never did have to commit perjury under duress. They settled out of court.

Too bad Red got away. I would have liked to have seen Auerbach and Cousy locked up together and the book thrown at them—a small one like *Gone With the Wind* or the Winston Churchill memoirs—for what they did to me in Poland.

I know the incident has been mentioned in Red's book and also Russell's, but I think I am entitled to my version, since it is my story and this is my book. I also know you would prefer the truth, and the only way that is possible is through me.

y high school graduation. Notice the handsome young man in the middle of the p row.

The good, old college days at Holy Cross.

It's my ball and nobody is going to take it from me.

Gee, I used to be able to get off the floor.

Once upon a time they could argue without me.

Two fond memories of my college basketball days: the MVP award at the Sugar Bowl and a bandaged knee.

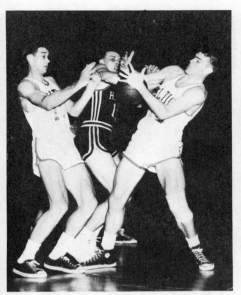

Those nasty NBA players just wouldn't let a young player have the ball without a struggle . . .

. . . and when I got it, there always was someone like Wilt Chamberlain around to pick on me.

I was a determined shooter from any angle and from anywhere, as you can readily see.

Nobody could ever say I didn't
have an outstanding floor game.

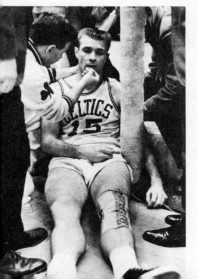

For some strange reason, Tom Meschery and Nate Thurmond expected me to shoot . . .

. . . So did Satch Sanders (16), setting a pick for me . . .

. . . and so did Bill Russell, jockeying with Wayne Embry for rebound position while Tom Hawkins fouls me, Mr. Referee.

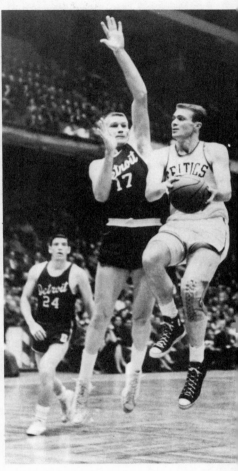

You can't always shoot from outside.

Hey, Cooz! Wait for me!

Just because some genius named me Ack-Ack, it didn't mean I shot all the time.

I loved to be where the action was ...

...but sometimes it was better that I not be.

Tom Meschery, the rookie, shows his respect for his NBA hero, Tommy Heinsohn.

Looks like a three-second violation to me.

A few of the championship teams. Can you identify the players and the years?

When Bill Russell and Bob Cousy weren't available, I was asked to make some awards.

John Havlicek and I join all the "old" Celtics at the NBA's twenty-fifth anniversary celebration.

A Boston reunion at the White House with President Kennedy.

Meet the press: Clif Keane, almost choked, and Bud Collins, almost obscured.

Sometimes the coach of the wonderful Boston Celtics got carried away.

We not only played together, we laughed together.

Before and during the great dialogue with Walter Brown over the threatened All-Star Game strike.

My playing career winds down to a precious few moments.

One of my proudest achievements, the first championship team I coached.

It started when a group of NBA players were invited to visit Europe for the State Department in 1964 after the Celtics had won for the seventh time in eight seasons. Auerbach was a veteran of such trips and the leader, so he took along me, Russell, K. C. Jones, Bob Pettit of the Hawks, Oscar Robertson and Jerry Lucas of the Royals, Tom Gola of the Knicks, and Cousy, then coaching at Boston College. First we went to the State Department for a briefing and met Dean Rusk, Secretary of State.

"I was the last of the midget centers," said the Secretary, a six-foot center at Davidson College. "They were all set shots in those days, no jump shots or hook shots. The scores were 18–12, 24–15. They shoot a lot better nowadays."

We were too diplomatic to ask how he could tell. Auerbach was acting as though he were the real Secretary of State, anyway. In those days of the Cold War, Red really got upset when he went overseas and saw the mileage the Russians got from political propaganda about their basketball team.

Reds made Red see red. This particular trip was to be his Mission to Moscow because, for the first time, the Russians indicated they might lift the curtain for an American pro team. Auerbach for many years had pushed the State Department to send over our best basketball representative—a team of pros—and finally succeeded.

Red put together maybe the greatest All-Star team of all time. He wasn't going to blow the opportunity to show the world which country owned basketball. As it turned out, we never got to Moscow. The provisional visas never were delivered because we slaughtered the Iron Curtain teams and Russia lost its enthusiasm to see us.

We visited President Johnson and then went for briefings on the Communist countries we would be visiting. There was an expert on each country and he cautioned about dealing in the black market and photographing military installations. He also provided a breakdown of the political attitudes, the social habits, the economics, the food, and everything that would provide an insight into the country.

They started with Poland, and the expert explained that only 5 per cent of the population were card-carrying Communists and the Polish people retained a fierce hatred for Germany because of two World Wars. I figured he was being a bit overdramatic, but since I was the only German in the group, I asked: "How much do they hate the Germans?"

He went to great lengths to explain how the Polish people showed their contempt for Germany in news articles and at every propaganda opportunity. Unknown to me, the wheels were turning when Auerbach and Cousy noticed my interest in Poland's attitude toward Germans. The schemers picked it up right away.

We arrived in Poland late at night and there was a bus and people from the Federation of Basketball waiting. Also meeting us was a woman sportswriter. She sat beside me on the bus and we talked. She didn't really know me, but she knew some of the others because they had played in the Olympics and some international basketball.

"Heinsohn, what is that?" she asked after we had been deeply into a pleasant conversation. I advised her I was of German extraction. That woman looked at me as though if she could have grabbed a gun, she would have shot me.

She stopped speaking, and I realized that fellow in the State Department had not been kidding. I then made a big mistake. When the guys got together, I told them the story about the woman sportswriter. That triggered it. Now every place we went after that—every airport, hotel, restaurant, or train station—they would run away from me yelling: "Deutsch! Deutsch!"

That became a running gag, so to speak. I had left myself wide open for it and then made myself even more vulnerable by getting involved in black marketing a few American dollars—exactly what we had been warned against. We were informed they might try to trap us, they'd search and bug rooms, and they'd even have people shadow us. Peter Lorre stuff, Iron Curtain style.

When we reached Warsaw, the rate of exchange was twenty-four zlotys to the American dollar, and the black-market rate was ninety-eight zlotys to the dollar. Everybody found the odds quite interesting and began wondering if there was anyone we knew familiar with the black market.

Somebody discovered that someone close to our basketball group had a connection. This Polish guy offered to change our money just to be hospitable. This was the way he worked: He would walk into your room, pull the shades down, put his finger to his lips to warn you not to talk, you'd follow him into the bathroom, hand him your investment, and away he went.

An hour or two later he was back with your money. He went through the same routine with the shades, no talking, the bathroom, and handed over the zlotys. He never said a word. Nervously in and out just like that.

Following that, I got hooked up with a native tennis player. He was anti-Communist because they had confiscated his property and left him practically a pauper. He was a very bitter man. He took me and K. C. Jones out for a tour of Warsaw one night, we had a few drinks, and he got bombed. At three o'clock in the morning, he stood in the middle of the square and screamed obscenities about the Communists in English.

That wasn't exactly something out of Stalin's course in etiquette. K.C. and I tried to choke him down and agreed, if anyone was following us, the KGB surely would receive a report on our friend and the company he kept. How would we ever know?

The next day we gave a clinic at the Palace of Culture, the biggest building in Warsaw at the time. In the course of staging the clinic on the twenty-fifth floor or something, I broke the crystal of the Accutron watch they had given me at the All-Star game that year. It was a unique watch that ran by battery and I loved it so much, I'm still wearing it.

I removed the battery and put it in my change pocket. I wrapped the watch in a T-shirt so the hands wouldn't be damaged and put it in my bag. Everytime I went to pay a check and pulled out money, the suspicious-looking battery appeared.

About five days went by and I couldn't find a new crystal, so I took the battery and wrapped it in the same T-shirt with the watch. We continued the trip and everywhere the guys still pointed at me and yelled: "Deutsch! Deutsch!"

Nothing was sacred or a deterrent. Not even when we went to Krakow and followed that with a visit to Auschwitz, where Nazi SS men had burned the bodies of as many as thirty thousand persons a night from 1940 to 1944. Where four to six million Jews and other prisoners had died. The Polish people at Auschwitz naturally stared at me when the fellows yelled: "Deutsch! Deutsch!"

You must gather by now that I figured I was not the most popular guy in Poland at that moment. I thought nothing of it, though, because there were no serious ramifications and the only harm done was to my feelings by the taunting from Auerbach, Cousy, and the other kibitzers.

I went back to the hotel after the Auschwitz incident and had to go into my suitcase for something. I discovered the watch in the T-shirt, but the battery was gone. I scratched my head. No battery. I concluded it must have fallen out someplace. I had searched the suitcase, thrown everything on the bed, but the battery was gone.

While I was trying to solve the mystery, there was a knock on the door. "Come in," I said. The door opened and a little guy with a trench coat walked in. "Tommy Heinsohn?" he asked. "Yes," I confessed. He whipped out his wallet and flashed a badge. "Get passport," he said, struggling with English. "Ask questions."

It all flashed through my mind. The black marketing. The tennis player blasting the Communists in the square. Auschwitz that day. They found the battery and they must think it some spying device. The battery was the key. Five seconds before I had gone through my bag for the battery. They must have searched the room and found it.

I decided there was no way I would go with that guy. Auerbach, Cousy, where are you? Tom Gola, my roomie, was shaving, and once in a while he would peek out at the visitor and then go back to shaving. The guy looked like something left over from a Humphrey Bogart movie, and I wasn't going with him. I was big enough to handle him.

Just then there was another knock on the door. Please, make it Auerbach or someone to help me. It was a bigger guy in another trench coat. He was around six-five and had his hands in his pocket. Ominous-looking. Like he had a gun in each hand.

"Tommy Heinsohn?" said the second guy. "Get passport. Ask questions." He circled behind me, and I was double-teamed. I know how Kareem Abdul-Jabbar feels with Cal Murphy in front and Rudy Tomjanovich behind. "They're going to shoot me," I said to myself.

They marched me out, and Gola hardly missed a beat shaving. He thought it was for real, too, and chose to remain inconspicuous and silent rather than go along with me and the Gestapo. "Tommy," I yelled as I went out the door. "Get Auerbach! Get the guys from the legation! These guys are arresting me!"

They took me through the lobby and out the hotel. We stopped in an alley. It was getting dark and, when I looked down the alley, it was pitch black. The two guys began arguing. Victor McLaglen was laughing and Peter Lorre was getting mad.

I knew they were discussing me because "Heinsohn" appeared in the conversation. Heinsohn in Polish is Heinsohm. They started into the alley. "Wait a minute," I said to myself. "Why are we going down this pitch-black alley? There is no way I'm doing that."

Visions of violence danced wildly in my head. I was going to get it in the alley or someplace. I worked out my game plan. I would grab Peter as Victor aimed the gun. No, that wouldn't be good because Victor could shoot me through the pocket of his trench coat. Besides, the gun in his pocket appeared to be so big, I figured the bullet would pass through Peter, the little body.

Okay, then. If they made a move, I'd hit 'em with a karate chop. The big guy made a move, and I was coiled like a cobra when he walked past and opened a door. I heard voices and music and looked in and saw a cafe. They led me into the place and I was happy to follow.

They sat me at a table and I felt even better than happy, whatever that is. People. Humans. They wouldn't dare do anything to me in front of people. Would they?

"You wait here," said Victor. "Be right back. Ask few questions." I sat for about ten minutes and smoked a few cigarettes when it finally dawned on me. What the hell was I sitting there for and waiting for those guys when I could make my getaway? Nobody could ever accuse me of being slow under pressure conditions.

I decided I'd get to hell out of there and find Auerbach because I knew those guys were coming after me as soon as they discovered I had skipped. I headed for the door to the alley and stopped. Wait a minute. That's why they left me. They want me to sneak into the alley and then they'd shoot me—claiming I was trying to escape. Justifiable murder.

If you had seen as many movies on the road as I had in my NBA career, you would be aware of all the tricks. The men's room. That's it. I'd seen that work for Bogart, I think. I went there but the windows were barred. I'd seen that happen to Bogart too.

I couldn't find another escape and went to my table to think some more. I was in the cafe for about twenty minutes and was panicking when in walked Auerbach, Cousy, Buddy Leroux, and the two Gestapos. I was so happy to see Red, I jumped and knocked over the table. The customers stared at the big, clumsy American. Who cared by then?

"Red," I screeched. "Those two SOBs with you are going to arrest me." Well, Red, Cousy, Leroux, and the two KGB men broke up. They laughed so hard, they almost fell to the ground I would have liked to have buried them all in. "You dirty bastards," was all I could say when I realized it had all been a joke.

Those dirty names had set me up beautifully. Peter Lorre and Victor McLaglen turned out to be the coaches of the teams we were playing. Their badges were from the Olympics. Their English was the result of a rehearsing they had received from Auerbach that day: "Tommy Heinsohn? Get passport. Ask questions."

The reason they had argued in the alley was because the original plan had called for them to drop me off at the police station and walk out. Red was the instigator, of course. As I suspected, the State Department briefing got him thinking, and his devious mind did the rest.

I made up my devious mind I would get even with Red and Gola, who wasn't even in on the plot, if it was the last thing I did.

8

IT WAS THE opening game of the 1964–65 season. Boston once more was favored to win the championship, having added seven-foot Mel Counts for bench strength as our No. 1 draft pick.

Our opponent was the New York Knicks with a number of new faces, such as a young man named Willis Reed, Bad News Barnes, Butch Komives, and Emmette Bryant. The Knicks had failed to make the playoffs again, so the Celtics represented the only real excitement for the first game.

Center jump. The crowd was buzzing. The referee tossed the ball. I was watching the tap when someone punched me in the back of the head. An NBA record. No possession, yet a punch had been thrown. I turned and Tom Gola was glaring at me.

"What did you do that for?" I asked. "You dirty bastard!" he said. "It had to be you." A good title for a song. However, that wasn't what he meant. Remember how I had promised to get Gola for copping out on me in Poland?

I did. Sooner than you think. Actually, Red had top priority, but he had escaped temporarily because of circumstances beyond my control. I had a neat idea worked out for him before our State Department trip ended. What better place for someone named Arnold Auerbach than Egypt, eh? Real diabolical.

It had been touchy for the State Department to get Auerbach cleared for Egypt. Unofficially Red was Jewish, officially he was the American coach of the American basketball team. In a sense, they sneaked Red into the country. The Egyptians knew it but they looked away—probably because Red wasn't much to look at, anyway.

Partly because of Red's ancestry, and partly because of the players, they had assigned General Thodios, the head of the secret police, to protect us. General Thodios was a former Olympic swimmer, basketball player, and competitor in other events. He had represented Egypt in five Olympic Games, a great athlete and a nice man.

I became very friendly with the general and his wife. I had been planning since Poland that, when we arrived in Egypt, something was going to happen to Mr. Auerbach. A Jew in Egypt was like a German in Poland. Perfect revenge.

I decided on something quick—nothing elaborate, like Red's tricks. I would hire an Arab, give him a rifle with blanks, and have him pop up on a roof when he saw Red coming. He would yell: "All right, you Jewish swine," and fire away. I would take whatever time necessary to teach the English words so I could have the pleasure of telling Red I had used some of his routine against him.

A good idea? General Thodios didn't think so. I figured if I went to tea with him and explained what I had in mind, he would get the Arab to fire the blanks and scare the hell out of Red. "You can't do that," was his reaction. "Why not?" I asked. "They *will* kill him." I told the general that his idea was better than mine.

He didn't think that was funny, so I agreed the idea of killing Red in cold blood was slightly ridiculous. "Maim him a little?" I suggested, compromising. Red escaped once again, but not Gola. I got him in Cairo on one of those spur-of-the-moment inspirations.

I couldn't forget Tommy's great human concern about being careful not to cut his neck while shaving as I was being arrested. Gola was a straight guy. Conservative, religious, family-oriented, a

solid citizen. He had brought his first movie camera on the trip to record everything for his wife and family back home. He would shoot
scenes in Poland, Yugoslavia, Egypt, and so forth.

We fell over watching him. He didn't know the first thing about
a camera. He would aim it and go: "Brrrp" and that was it. A quick
burst. Three frames of a cathedral, 4½ frames of Auschwitz. He had
no idea what he was doing. No one told him, naturally.

He brought along about sixty rolls of films and, at the rate he
was going, he had enough to go around the world a few times. When
we got to Egypt, after the Iron Curtain countries, he was working on
his fortieth frame. Could you imagine him shooting *The Godfather?*

Tommy had gone to school with the manager of the Hilton that
was on one side of the Nile while we were staying across the river—
like in Brooklyn. His friend extended us the courtesy of using the
Hilton pool and discovering that the pyramids and the Sphinx did
not represent the only beautiful sights in Egypt.

Every stewardess from the Scandinavian airlines was based at
the Hilton. It was some oasis. In addition to those busy bikinis, the
show in the rooftop room offered some great-looking Eurasian girls
who had just finished a tour in Las Vegas. More beauties in bikinis
for the pool. I had to admit it was a lot better than watching Chamberlain, Russell, or Jerry West running around in shorts.

We sat ourselves at the bar and had a great time watching the
girlie parade. There had to be about a hundred in bikinis around the
pool. Gola, Lucas, Pettit, Cousy, and I couldn't find anything better
to do for some reason.

Tommy had to leave because his friend called him into the
office. He left his super camera with the zoom lens on the bar. The
lights clicked in my mind. Gola had taken the camera along to show
home movies of the trip to his family. I would see to it that Tommy
would bring home shots that lasted a little longer than four frames.

He had told me he was planning to invite all of his relatives over
for the viewing. Everyone is entitled to one mistake, and Tommy
made it by telling me that. I picked up his camera, with which I had
mucho experience and was fairly good, and proceeded to zoom in on
the most important and attractive parts of every girl in those teenie-
weenie bikinis. In living color. In living flesh. For Gola and home
consumption. Zooming in. Zooming out. Zooming in.

Down. Sideways. Upside down. What have you. I felt obliged to at least do that little favor for my friend Gola, who didn't know how to handle a camera. How would it look if Mrs. Gola sat there with the kids and the relatives and all they saw were three frames of a pyramid or four frames of a desert lizard or five frames of a dinky camel?

I finished three quarters of the roll for Tommy, put the camera down, and never said a word when he returned. I never knew what happened until a few months later in October, when he greeted me with a shot behind my head I then knew I had made him a big cameraman with his wife and family.

"I went home," he told me, "and had all my relatives at the house. My in-laws. My mother and father. My uncle the priest. Here I am watching the cathedral, the four frames of this and the four frames of that until we get to the pyramids."

I was busting inside by then. "We get to the pryamids," he continued, "and all of a sudden there's a quick shift and every bub in the whole world, zeroed up close, comes on the screen. You, you . . ."

That took care of Gola. I had to wait until the tail end of the season to finally land Auerbach, the big fish. The best part of it was that the State Department briefing supplied the basis for my hooking him.

For the momentous occasion, I chose San Francisco, the home of the Warriors and Chamberlain, Thurmond, Tom Meschery, with whom I had had a wonderful fight when he was a rookie, and Guy Rodgers. That was the season in which Wilt was traded to the Philadelphia 76ers the night of the All-Star game in St. Louis.

The reason San Francisco wound up as the historic site for the Auerbach revenge was because there was a waitress in the Sheraton Palace who hated Red with a passion. One of many, of course. She had wonderful taste, she liked me. She was in her late 50s and took a motherly interest in me.

I tried to convince her Red was not a bad guy once you got to know him, but then I realized what I was saying. She hated Red, she spoke with an accent that sounded German, and the episode in Poland flashed back.

"How much do you really hate Red?" I asked. "I really don't like him at all," she said. "He's rough. Never smiles. Always in a hurry." My mind worked fast. I recalled how Red had given some woman we had met during the State Department briefing a lot of money to buy an alligator bag when we were in Egypt. She was Egyptian but had become an American citizen.

She had known a special shop that sold alligator pocketbooks, but Red had never received them. The hotel waitress was assigned to represent that lost woman with Red's lost pocketbook. I told the waitress to call Auerbach's room and tell him she was Naja something or other—I forget the name now.

"Tell him," I told her, "you are happy you finally found him. You lost his address. You didn't know where to send the pocketbook. You picked up the paper and saw his name and, since you happened to be in town with your husband and just happened to have the pocketbook, you want to deliver it."

I suggested she tell Red there was only one problem. She was leaving to catch a plane and would like to come over right away and drop the bag off in his room. I assured her Red would not allow a woman in his room and would suggest meeting her some other place.

I told her the street corner where she should meet Red so he could get the bag. It worked exactly as I thought, and he arranged to meet Naja a few blocks from the hotel. He left the Sheraton Palace, walked to Market Street, and stood there waiting.

I packed four or five guys from the team in a car and drove to the spot and we began laughing when we saw him. We kept driving around the block and he was sweating and cursing and probably saying: "Where the hell is that woman?" He wanted that alligator bag.

We had plucked a ratty old bag out of some garbage can during our rounds and we couldn't stand it anymore. We opened a window, slowed down, and yelled: "Red!" He looked and we flipped the bag at him. "Here's your pocketbook, Red." I got even with him but he never got even with the woman of the alligator bag. She disappeared forever with his money.

It was a quickie and not too ingenious, but it worked to my satisfaction. Red could be quick on the draw if necessary. He didn't have to work out an intricate plot to get me, his old whipping boy. For example, there was the day I call My Bad Day. Everyone has had a bad day, and this was mine.

I measure everything in life against this particular cluster of circumstances. I woke up one morning anxious to find out about several insurance cases on which I had worked and strained. Early in my career as a Celtic, someone had written a story about what I might do when my playing days were over. I had said I would like to latch onto some business right away, possibly insurance, so I could stake out a future.

I received a call from an insurance man who said he had read the story and would like to meet if I was interested. We met and had a long conversation. He turned out to be a most aware and convincing man—so convincing that by the time I walked out of his office, I had purchased twenty thousand dollars of life insurance myself.

He was the one who got me involved in the insurance business, and on this particular day, a few years into my Celtic career, I had a few big deals pending. I went to the breakfast table, opened the mail, and discovered I hadn't closed one case. I had lost a considerable amount of potential money. I wasn't hungry anymore, which must have shocked Diane and the kids.

I left the house and headed for the studio to do my radio show before practice. I was depressed because I had invested a lot of time during the summer on the insurance cases and had nothing to show for it. I pulled up in front of the radio station and there were no parking spots.

I had been through that before during the many years of doing my show. It was a ten-minute program over WAAB that I had from my second year in the league until I quit playing. I would give the sports as part of the regular six o'clock news and tape interviews on the road.

Bernie Waterman, who used to broadcast the Big Ten and Notre Dame football games, had purchased the five-thousand-watt station and hired me as his sports ace. I read the stuff off the wires for the first couple of weeks and then one day I walked into the studio and there was this chick with short shorts, a white T-shirt, and soaking wet.

"This is your guest for tonight," Bernie announced. "They had the hydroplane races at Lake Quinsigomond today and she set the Class B record. We had her brought right over."

I had assumed that. I didn't think Bernie had dropped her into a tub just to make a radio show seem realistic. I took him aside because I wanted to ask him something relatively important in private. "What the hell is a hydroplane?" was my question.

Bernie told me to forget about that and just sit with the girl and do some background work. We decided that it would be wise for her to explain why hydroplaning provided the best sports opportunity for a woman to compete on the same level as a man. We were ready to go live.

I started the show with a few routine questions, then asked the one we had prepared about woman vs. man. She didn't say a word. I began to panic. She put her hand over the mike and said: "I didn't understand the question." In spite of the rehearsal, no less.

I repeated the question and she went on to answer it, finally. I asked the next question on my list: "Have you taken any bad spills?" She began answering, and I did what any novice sportscaster would have done under the circumstances: I didn't listen carefully as I searched my list for the next question. Consequently, I never really paid attention to her reply: "Well, once the boat nosed over and I almost broke my back.. Another time I almost drowned."

As soon as I detected she had finished, I said: "Well, that's wonderful." Then I realized what she had said, so I picked it up from there by saying: "Oh, what I mean is that it's wonderful you're all in one piece—and a very nice piece at that."

That was one of my cherished ad-libs at the radio station. It was far from my agitated mind, however, the day of My Bad Day as I drove around looking for a spot for my car. It was getting late and I couldn't find a damned thing. Everyone seemed to have driven to work that day and gotten to the parking area before me.

I went to the no-parking loading zone and left the car there because I was only going to be in the studio about twenty minutes to tape my show. I went upstairs and was delayed when a machine broke down. It took me another twenty minutes to cut the show and, when I got downstairs, there was a parking ticket.

There was another complication. I would now be late for practice because the Boston Garden was about an hour away. I jammed my foot on the gas pedal and proceeded to go at a heady pace because I was steaming.

I looked out the window and what did I see? A state trooper. He invited me to pull over to the side of the road and stop. There was no RSVP enclosed, so I accepted on the spot. "Where do you think you're going?" he asked. "I'm Tommy Heinsohn, I'm with the Celtics, I'm late for practice," I rattled off.

I got a speeding ticket on top of the parking ticket. I was really ticked off. I was late for practice, rushed to get taped, and, when I arrived upstairs, Auerbach, the compassionate, advised me that it would cost ten dollars. By then I was numb.

I had a miserable practice, and Red grumbled about that. This wasn't right. That wasn't right. I was happy when the workout ended. We had practiced at Northeastern University, and I went to my locker and discovered someone had broken in and stolen my wallet with all my money, my draft card, and my credit cards.

I sat there and wondered: "What more can happen to me on this day?" I must have had an unusually sad expression for such a kind face because Auerbach walked over and asked what was wrong.

I cited chapter and verse. "In addition," I said, "you fined me and then my wallet's stolen with everything else." I really wasn't looking for sympathy—not from Auerbach. He surprised me, though, which, if I had any brains, should have made me suspicious immediately.

"Look," he said, "that's a bad day. What you ought to do—nothing relaxes me more than a cigar. You're just gonna relax if you smoke this cigar." He handed me a roman candle and I put it in my pocket. I was too overwrought and slightly shocked by Red's generosity to think clearly.

I was mad at the world as I headed back for home in Worcester, where we lived before we bought a new home in South Natick. I got about halfway when I began talking to myself, for a change. "What the hell are you getting so angry about?" I asked. "I'll be alright," I answered. "I'll take Red's advice. I'll smoke his cigar and relax."

I stopped at a red light and took out the cigar. I stuck it in my mouth and lit it. I took two puffs and the damn thing exploded. I was so mad, I could have taken the rifle I wanted to give that Arab in Egypt and shot Auerbach on the spot—with real bullets.

I never acknowledged that I smoked the loaded cigar. "Hey," he said when I saw him at practice the next day, "how did you like that cigar?" I told him I had never smoked it but had given it to somebody. I didn't want to give him the pleasure—only a loaded cigar of my own.

I set him up by feeding him cigars for the next four months. I wasn't too obvious. It would be once a week or every two weeks. It cost me a dollar and sometimes a dollar and a half but I would tell him I picked up a good one for him at a banquet.

At first he looked at both ends to see if it was loaded. He reached the point where he finally trusted me and lit the cigar without inspecting it. I was ready to pick my spot. It came when we were practicing at Northeastern for another playoff.

The setting was perfect because the media were there and Red was distracted by a press conference. He had all the reporters around when I handed him my cigar, revenge brand. He nodded, put it in his mouth, but didn't have a match.

I was on the fringe of a circle that must have included twenty newspapermen. I wanted to see the whole thing but was careful not to be too obvious. Red was busy telling everyone how great the Celtics were going to be and how they were going to do this and that, meanwhile fumbling for a match.

I began to panic. For want of a match, I was about to blow the opportunity after all my investment of time and money. What do I do now? I grabbed my lighter and worked my way closer to him. "Red, whatsa matter?" I said, innocently. "Gotta match?" he asked, conveniently.

Magnificent. It couldn't have been better. My cigar and my match. He took two puffs and said: "We will defeat the Seventy . . ." Boom! No more press conference. He chased me out of the locker room and up the stairs.

They had some weird senses of humor on the Celtics. I have a picture on the wall in my den that is a classic example of what I mean. It shows Tom Meschery of the Warriors swinging at me, I have backed away making him miss, and Jim Loscutoff, our hatchet-man, is standing a few feet away with hands on hips, grinning.

Right. Your reaction was the same as mine. Why would Loscy, a notorious enforcer who had muscles he hadn't used yet, consider it funny that someone on the other team was trying to deck me, Tommy Heinsohn, his roomie?

He forgot all the things I had done for him. How patient I had been when his wife called at 9:00 A.M. Boston time and woke us up at 6:00 A.M. Los Angeles time to tell him she had just purchased a fire engine for their summer camp. She couldn't wait. You'd think she was going to a fire.

Loscy had an explanation why he had laughed at Meschery's violence. He said he knew players from San Francisco were notorious for walking away, then turning suddenly and firing a sneak punch. Meschery, who had played at St. Mary's in California, had done that and Loscy had smiled because he had guessed right.

That eased the pain a little for me but not for Meschery. He received the worst of it in every respect. It was not one of my prouder fights because Tom was not a bad soul. He was a poet, in fact. Now, why would a poet and an artist, both aesthetic and sensitive by nature, resort to such violence?

First, let me give you an illustration of the poetry that emanated from the cranium of Meschery. This was symbolically named *The Fight:*

> *The first guy to get hit*
> *head spins to the side*
> *and comes up bleeding*
> *Cameras close in, bulbs flash*
> *announcers high pitch*
> *blow by blow*
> *back to hometown*
> *Fists curve crooked arcs*
> *flicker like candles*
> *and snuff out. . . .*
> *Crack!*
> *The arena shatters*
> *into a million splinters*
> *that last soprano punch*
> *sending fans flying.*

Not bad poetry for a basketball jock, which helps if you can fight when that's what you have in mind. That was what Meschery had in mind, no doubt, that night in March of 1962 at the Boston Garden. He was a rookie with the Philadelphia Warriors, a franchise later to be sold by Eddie Gottlieb and to become the San Francisco Warriors.

When Tom entered the league that season, one of the first things he had mentioned to the media was that he wanted to play like Tommy Heinsohn. I had been his hero through his college career at St. Mary's and he had patterened his moves and game after my style. All year this kid played me toe-to-toe, and there hardly was a word between us. Nothing nasty, anyway.

It was near the end of the season and the game meant nothing, but Philadelphia vs. Boston was hot stuff in those days because of Chamberlain and Russell. We already had clinched first place, and the Warriors had locked up second. I grabbed a rebound and Al Attles grabbed my arm and knocked the ball loose.

The refs gave them possession and I filed an objection in my own poetic way. "Why don't you call those things?" I screamed. "The guy grabbed me by the arm. Call it, will you please? You saw the play."

Objection overruled. Meschery turned to his hero and snarled: "Don't you ever stop bitching?" Fickle, wasn't he? I turned around and very politely, as was my custom, told him what he could do to himself. I don't think he could have gotten any madder if I had refused to give him my autograph.

A little later, I was driving toward the basket, and Meschery threw himself at me and knocked me into the support. They gave me two shots, which was good enough for me but not him. I walked toward the foul line and, as I turned, I saw him coming.

I waited. He came up to me, looked, didn't say anything, and made a move as though leaving. Out of the corner of my eye I saw the punch coming. I pulled back and the jet stream from the miss almost knocked me down. I don't know who was sorry more, Meschery or me, because I hit him so hard, he required seven stitches to close the cut on his left eyebrow.

They told me Meschery actually wanted to come back and fight after he was repaired. They wouldn't let him so he blew off steam in the papers. "My only regret is that I missed the punch," he said. I appreciated it, though.

"Heinsohn's constant complaining to the refs," he continued, "all season long about being fouled and the way he smirks at you and some things he says have been bugging me. We had a few words, again, and I just got tired of taking his guff. The guy is like no one else in this league. I can take guys that rough you up as long as they don't throw it back in your face. I figure if a guy is going to give it out he should know how to take a little in return and keep his mouth shut.

"But not Heinsohn. You foul him and he moans to the refs the rest of the game. They say he's an alright guy off the court but I only know him on the court and don't like the way he acts. I admire the guy as a player. He's a great one. But his whole personality leaves me with a great distaste."

What an ingrate. I allowed him to worship me and he talked

about his hero that way. I was thrown out of the game for the disturbance and so was Auerbach for defending me too loudly and descriptively. Red was strange that way. He became angry whenever anyone picked on me. He considered it an infringement of copyright.

Maybe I didn't treat Meschery fairly. Maybe I should have called time and told him the facts of NBA life or what had happened to me a few weeks earlier in Los Angeles in a small disagreement with Rudy LaRusso, a physical forward out of Dartmouth by way of Brooklyn.

LaRusso many years later was to be involved in one of the wildest fights ever seen in Madison Square Garden. He took a swing at Willis Reed, two L.A. guys grabbed Willis from behind, and Willis then swung at everyone in a Laker uniform. John Block got off the bench for a closer look at the action and had his nose broken. Darrell Imhoff, insisting he was a peacemaker, got an eyebrow busted open. The referees stopped the fight in the first round.

My particular night with LaRusso started when Rudy went after Cousy, something of a mismatch. Loscy and I were Cousy's volunteer protectors. We knew he couldn't fight and we surely didn't want to lose the guy passing the ball.

Rudy decided to take over when Frank Selvy, his teammate, closed in on Cousy. LaRusso moved in behind Cousy and I moved in behind LaRusso and hit him in the back of the head. Loscutoff stepped in and hooked Rudy with one arm and cut off Jim Krebs, the Lakers' huge center. There were a few shoves and swings before the referees gained control.

No one was thrown out and time was called to cool tempers. In our huddle, Red told us to forget it and concentrate on the game because we were only in the first half. I can guess what went on in the Laker huddle.

On the first play when the game resumed, someone on our side took a shot, and I went tearing for the offensive rebound as usual. The Laker defense opened up like the Red Sea had for Moses, and Krebs, under the boards, let me have an elbow right in the face. Hooray for Hollywood!

I hit the floor on my head and was knocked out. I didn't really know where I was until they attended to me in the dressing room. They insisted that I go to the hospital for X rays to determine if I had a concussion.

I was groggy but not totally out of it. Ernie Vandeweghe, the old Knick player, was the Lakers' doctor at the time. He offered to drive me to the hospital and I ended up sitting in front with his wife, holding my hand and pacifying me. She was Kay Colleen Hutchins, a former Miss America. If I had to go, that was the way.

"Wait'll we get them in Boston," announced Auerbach the Terrible after the game. I had my own ideas. I cut out the stories the next day and stuffed them in my bag. I wanted to be sure I had something fresh to motivate me the next time I saw Krebs. It was the only time in all my playing days I ever made up my mind to get someone.

My nature was to forget about a fight and play the next game. I never held a grudge against anyone. I was Mr. Nice Guy until I met Krebs' elbow. I wanted those stories to read as a fresh reminder just before I went out to play the Lakers again.

The schedule was perfect. Los Angeles would play us in Boston the final game of the regular season with the races over. I carried those stories around for three weeks but never got to use them. The night before I planned to get Krebs, I had the fight with Meschery and was threatened with suspension if I didn't play nice, not fight.

As I have said many times, I was an emotional player. I thrust myself deeply into a ball game. I was intense and it showed on my face. I would run like hell for six or seven minutes and get a little tired.

I would then push myself, with the contrast so obvious it appeared as though I were acting. It really wasn't a performance, just natural hills and valleys that led Buster Sheary and Red Auerbach to feel I needed motivation.

That is how I became Red's whipping boy. He felt he had to wind up the Tommy Heinsohn doll, whereupon I would have the last word before the Celtics stormed out of the dressing room to conquer the basketball world.

No one would go through the door until I had delivered my inspirational message, which for drama, impact, and content ranked with President Roosevelt's declaration of war against Japan, Winston Churchill's Dunkirk speech, and President Kennedy's "Ask not what your country can do for you, ask what you can do for your country."

Red would finish his pregame talk. The players would jump off their seats and clap their hands, ready to go. Then they would freeze and look at me. No one moved out until I spoke. I would stretch out all six-seven of me and shout: "Let's win this % ※ *＋% ※&% @ ※ game!" For that I went to college? We won most of our games, didn't we?

I wonder what would have happened to the Celtics if I had developed lockjaw? They'd probably still be sitting in the dressing room waiting for me to say something. I was the dressing room inspiration; Russell was the inspiration once the game started.

Not that I wasn't capable of drawing attention because of the dramatic flair I must have developed playing the lead in high school operettas. When I got hit, I would fall and stay down while the other players walked away and and prepared to resume without me. One time I was knocked down, remained on the floor waiting for the call as the play went the other way, jumped up when we got the rebound, and took a long pass for a layup.

Some accused me of being dramatic solely because of the faces I made. A sort of Lon Chaney, Sr., with a thousand faces of my own. I just happen to have an interesting face for basketball. When I became coach of the Celtics, they seemed to feel my expressions were unusual and worthy of artistic reproduction, like a good painting. They concentrated the television cameras more on me than any other coach because of my glares, stares, anguish, and other facial extensions of my emotions.

As a coach, I never say half the things to referees other coaches do but I developed the bad reputation. Once I had to ask Auerbach to sit near me so he could evaluate my dialogue with the officials, and he agreed I was being misunderstood. Everyone knows, of course, how objective Red can be when it comes to referees.

I do get disturbed, but I never lose sight of what is going on. I am in total control of my senses. I know what I am saying to the officials and they know it. No one can say he ever saw me get mad at one of my players—publicly, anyway. Some people think I am acting when I jump up and take a walk. I just don't know how anyone can believe that I am now an actor or was when I was playing.

That happened, you know. I am the only player in the history of the NBA to ever be awarded an Emmy. One day during practice for the playoffs, Walter Brown walked in with two girls. Auerbach stopped the workout and pretended to be as puzzled over the intrusion as I or the other Celtics, though he was in on it, naturally.

One girl was private secretary for the president of the Boston & Maine Railroad, the other a friend she took to the games with the company's season tickets. They had approached Walter Brown and told him they wanted to present me with a special award.

They carried a paper bag and proceeded to seriously make a presentation to someone. "We are here today," said the private secretary, "to honor in a most distinguished fashion the great accomplishments of one of you gentlemen." That really confused us because we didn't know which gentleman she had in mind—there were so many.

"Without exception," she continued, "this gentleman has achieved the utmost in the performance of his craft." She gave it a big buildup and then removed the trophy from the paper bag. Later I found out that they originally wanted a hamhock for the award but that was considered too undignified and undeserving in view of the recipient.

Those girls actually contacted the Emmy people and received permission to produce a replica. "We'd like to present this award to Tommy Heinsohn," she finally announced, ending the suspense. It was entirely serious and precise up to that point, except she failed to ask for the Price, Waterhouse envelope.

Everyone broke up. I smiled and did four faints for the occasion. Then they asked for an encore. When you are recognized as Actor of the Year, could you do less?

9

"HEINSOHN IS THE No. 1 heel in my long association with sports." Walter Brown, owner of the Boston Celtics and a man I deeply respected, said that about me after the NBA Players' Association almost struck the 1964 All-Star game.

That was the only bad experience I had in nine years with the organization as a player and my years as coach since I took the job after Bill Russell quit. It happened on January 14, and Walter Brown, a sensitive man and highly principled individual, did not talk to me the rest of the season. Everytime he saw me move into his row to watch the first game of a doubleheader, he would get up and walk away.

"I'm burned up and I'm sore about it," he had said after the players called off their threatened strike just before game time. "It was a fine way for any of my players to treat me. My first obligation is to those people up in the seats."

Walter Brown was talking about Tommy Heinsohn, Bill Russell, and Sam Jones, the three Celtics in the game. He couldn't believe any of his players would even think of striking the All-Star game, knowing what it meant to him. He had been the father of the game, the one who had the vision and persistence to convince the other owners to let him promote the first one in the Boston Garden on March 2, 1951.

No one but Walter Brown had faith in the game and he, understandably, considered it his baby through the years. He expected his deep loyalty and attachment to be respected and understood by his players and everyone in the organization. We had let him down. More specifically, Tommy Heinsohn had let him down.

I understood why he must have been hurt and considered me ungrateful at the time. He had always been generous. He had adjusted my contract and gave me a two-thousand-dollar raise in its second year before I had even played a game for the Celtics. He never hassled about money.

It was customary for the players to avoid Auerbach's tough negotiations and drop in to see Walter Brown. Some Celtics left their contracts on his desk and let him fill in the figures. They trusted him and they never got less than a fair deal but invariably more.

Satch Sanders would get trapped one-on-one with Red and discovered that NYU had not fully prepared him for the confrontation. Sanders improvised because he was an unusually alert individual, as Harvard learned when it researched him and then made him its basketball coach.

Satch came up with a funny way of dealing with Auerbach, tougher with money than with referees. He walked in on Red carrying a sign that read: "It's not enough." Auerbach talked and Satch listened. When the figure became reasonable and acceptable, Satch flipped the sign and it read: "Okay, I'll take it."

I had more of a personal relationship with Walter Brown than anyone. He had so much faith in me, he actually allowed me to handle his estate. One day we were driving home from visiting someone in the hospital and he asked about my insurance business. I explained that I handled estates and then somehow got the inspiration to ask if he might be interested.

He said: "Yes," and that led to a unique situation since, in helping Walter Brown draw up his estate, I possessed privileged information as to what would be Red Auerbach's participation in the Boston Celtics' property. I guess it mostly was because of what Walter

Brown expected of me under those circumstances that made him so angry. He felt that I, as president of the Players' Association, knowing his attachment for the All-Star game, never should have allowed anything to disturb the fourteenth renewal, in Boston.

He had been a stanch supporter of the Players' Association at a time when Cousy, the first president, was trying to establish a base of recognition. Walter Brown had been a liberal force in the anti-union wilderness—at a time when Fred Zollner threatened to fire any and all Fort Wayne Pistons who joined the Association. By contrast, Walter Brown actually paid my way to attend the league meetings as a player representative, when almost all his fellow owners were anti-association.

He was a man of high quality who asked little in return other than a degree of loyalty or gratitude. He was a man who wanted to do right by everybody. I was aware of that. That is why I went to him when it appeared as though there would be a problem at the All-Star game.

It had been brewing for years. When Cousy quit as head of the Association, I took over and inherited the problems. As an individual dealing with insurance and estates, I helped establish the pension plan that led to total indifference from the owners. The player representatives, consequently, decided they would hold a meeting the day before the All-Star game in Boston and devise forceful action.

The owners had ordered Maurice Podoloff, when he was commissioner, to stall and commit nothing. At times, they had been extremely insulting, letting us sit in the lobby of a hotel where they were meeting and refusing to see us. Even with the new regime of Walter Kennedy, there had been no noticeable progress toward a pension plan, and the players indicated they had been ignored enough.

I felt obligated to alert Walter Brown. "I anticipate a problem at your All-Star game," I told him. "If you are going to run a banquet, the players are planning to run one of their own because they want to use it as a meeting in regard to the pension."

He got upset at the word "pension." "I don't have a pension," he said, "why should you guys have one?" That didn't sound like him but I reminded him, anyway, that the players had been anxious to work out a pension plan with the owners for a long time. I alerted him once more at a later date about the impending trouble but I had no idea at the time what form it would take.

There was a blizzard that year and the players had trouble

reaching Boston the day before the game, so the banquets were ruined. Players came by train and dogsled. We kept a meeting running all day to accommodate those who straggled in from different parts of the country.

It was unanimously agreed that there would be no All-Star game unless we received a written commitment on a pension plan. We had been turned down in the morning by Walter Kennedy and Fred Zollner, representing the Board of Governors and the pension committee.

We knew Zollner's attitude toward the Association, which gave us a fair idea as to the result. Walter Kennedy was new at the game but knew we had tried to talk with the Board of Governors in New York in October of that season and had been ignored. We left humiliated, angry, and determined to establish our dignity, at the least.

At six o'clock the night of the All-Star game, after we had met with all the players, Bob Pettit and I went to Commissioner Kennedy's hotel room and informed him we would not play without a pension guarantee. We asked for a meeting with the owners before the game or else. We were not militant people by nature or background but were forced to challenge the owners' one-way attitude in some way.

I, for one, was not including Walter Brown because I knew him as a fair and reasonable man who would not use and abuse power for power's sake like the others. Still, in my position, I took out insurance, like a good insurance man, by having every player representative in the league give me written approval of our actions. If it got a little sticky, I wanted everyone to know he was on record with his signature.

I did it for self-protection because I had the most to lose with Walter Brown. I was putting myself in the middle with the guy I loved, and in Boston, my hometown. I had enough experience with human nature to know that when it got too hot, some would sneak out of the kitchen.

Walter Kennedy came to our dressing room and told us he couldn't gather all the owners together to act on our ultimatum before the game. He was informed we would not play under those conditions; the game would not go on national television as scheduled. The point was made that we would ruin the league with our obstinance, and we reminded the commissioner as to how we had been trying to talk with the owners but they hadn't the decency to even acknowledge we existed.

Commissioner Kennedy was feeling his way around the league at the time. He didn't know all the owners or players. He did recognize it was a serious situation for his eight owners. At first he wouldn't talk because Larry Fleisher was in the room. I had hand-selected Fleisher as our labor negotiator, and Commissioner Kennedy felt that disqualified him because Fleisher was only a representative.

We took care of that when the commissioner left to see if he could deliver our message to all eight owners. We elected Fleisher an officer of the Association right then and gave him official status. Meanwhile, several owners tried to pull their players out of the room to break the threatened strike.

They attempted to force their way in but we had anticipated that and assigned a strong policeman to the door. I told the little Irish cop not to let anyone in unless he received my okay. He was a sweet old guy in his sixties, and I'll bet he never had a more difficult assignment than keeping Bob Short out when he was threatening Elgin Baylor and Jerry West.

Short, owner of the Lakers, managed to send word to West and Baylor to get their fannies on the court if they knew what was good for them. They somehow knew what was good for them and remained with rest of the players. Baylor was the superstar at the time and it was to his credit that he stood up. If he or anyone had backed down, it would have been all over.

"Tell Bob Short," was the message Baylor sent his boss through the cop at the door, "I'm not moving and he'd better not start threatening me." Short happened to be there the earliest among the owners, so he had taken it upon himself to try to break us. He came up a little short, though I must admit some players wavered.

Chamberlain insisted we play the game from the moment he showed. He obviously forgot that I had his autograph on a piece of paper that officially endorsed whatever action we chose to take. If he would like to see it, I think I still have it in my files.

Commissioner Kennedy saved everything by assuring us he would convince the owners to provide the pension plan if we played the game. That was at eight twenty-five, and the game was scheduled for nine o'clock. We asked him to step outside while we met again.

There were discussions as to whether we should trust the com-missioner or whether we should not play until the owners guaranteed us the plan. There was a faction that still didn't want to play. It finally came back to me because, as chairman of the meeting, I had listened and waited for my chance to say something.

I made a plea for the game to be played. I explained that I thought we had made our point with Commissioner Kennedy and we should trust him until we found out otherwise, then we would take stronger action the next time. I think I swung the vote to play.

I sincerely believed we had spotlighted the issue and there was no practical sense in antagonizing the owners, the fans, and everyone unnecessarily. I had an influence on the decision and, at eight fifty-five, or five miutes before the game was to go on national television, we informed Commissioner Kennedy we had accepted his proposal.

We had five minutes to shoot around, and the East went out and beat the West, 111–107. It was a pleasant ending to a grueling day until Walter Brown let me know how he felt about what had just happened to him, his invited guests, and his game. He had been the host, and to put it bluntly, he blew his cork.

Auerbach came to me before the game and told me Walter was upset. I was so disturbed by that, I didn't remember playing. I scored five baskets from memory. I felt horrible because Walter Brown was accusing me of being insensitive or disloyal or something.

It was the one time that playing for the Celtics was not fun and games. I didn't want to talk with my wife or anyone. I went to the Sheraton Copley, where we were staying overnight because we were leaving early the next day for an out-of-town game, and headed for the bar.

Max Winter was standing there. Max, now owner of the Minne-sota Vikings, had been the original owner of the Minneapolis Lakers and had sold the team to Short. As if I weren't upset enough, Max proceeded to call me a traitor, a disgrace to the game and to the loy-alty Walter Brown had shown me.

I told Max I had done what I had to do. He told me how much I had upset Walter Brown. I found out how much the next day when I picked up the paper and saw Walter Brown accuse me of being the biggest heel he'd ever seen in sports.

I not only figured I had blown a beautiful relationship with a beautiful person but also my career in Boston. He was an impulsive individual and was capable of doing almost anything. I was depressed, and the statements in the paper did not make me feel any better.

I knew if I didn't take the initiative, Walter Brown, a stubborn Irishman, would lose respect for me, if he had any left. I discussed it with Auerbach and he appointed himself my diplomatic representative. "I will talk to Walter," said Red. "Give it a few days to cool off."

We went to Baltimore for a game and it became worse inside. I found it difficult sleeping. I told Red once more I wanted to speak with Walter Brown, and Red asked for another day or two. He finally arranged for me to come in for a meeting.

I felt like I was going to my draft board when I walked into the Celtics' office in a wing of the Boston Garden. Someone had alerted the media, and the place was jammed. I was surprised. I had been one of the lesser luminaries on the team and never expected the reporters to be that interested in me.

I was a star for a day. I had to hurt Walter Brown to finally gain some recognition. Throughout my career with the Celtics, there always was Cousy, Russell, and someone else. With them on the team, I became Mr. Matter-of-Fact, no matter what I did.

I tell one story whenever someone asks for an example. We played a game with the Lakers in Seattle and it might have been my greatest performance. I think I scored forty-seven points, grabbed many rebounds and just played a super game.

The next day I bought a paper and the story was devoted to Cousy, Russell, Sharman, and Baylor; Elgin had rejoined the Lakers that day after having met some military obligation. The last line mentioned me. Tommy Heinsohn also had played.

Right there I knew what my role would be on the Celtics. "I guess," I told Gene Conley, "I'm never gonna be a star." I learned to live with that the same way as had Sam Jones and Frank Ramsey. Ramsey never played in an All-Star game because the rule restricted it to a maximum of three players representing one team, yet I sincerely believe he belongs in the Hall of Fame on ability that was not recognized through no fault of his own.

Therefore, I was shocked when I saw all the newspapermen waiting for me outside Walter Brown's office. It looked like my wake or the greatest story of all time. I was apprehensive, naturally, but

somewhat relieved after I had digested all the remarks Walter Brown
made to the newspapers the day of our meeting.

"I don't know what will transpire in our meeting," he said, "but
I'll say this—I have no intention of apologizing to anybody." Someone reminded him that I had said the owners had favored a player-
assistance plan two years previously and failed to go through with it.

A fair observation? "Regardless of what anybody says," replied
Walter Brown, face getting red, "the players voted to pull a strike at
a most critical time on Tuesday. They're just trying to hammer us
over the head."

Someone, in the normal pursuit of duty, then asked if Tommy
Heinsohn might be traded. I needed someone to think of that at that
time. "No, I wouldn't trade him," he snapped. "But if I had a team
in Honolulu, I'd ship him there." At least I wouldn't be traded.

That made me feel a little better—like avoiding the gas chamber
to sit in the electric chair. I walked into the office and Walter Brown
was sitting behind his desk—huffing, puffing, groaning, and
grumbling. I explained I had to come to tell him I had no idea what
was going to happen at the All-Star game and I had gone to him to
alert him to the situation.

I pointed out that there was nothing personal, that I had acted
solely in my role as president of the Association as he might as a
member of the Board of Governors. I was trying to reason with him,
not cop a plea. I could have explained how I had used my influence
on the players not to strike, but I wasn't looking for sympathy—just
understanding. I felt that would be bribing him. Each man has his
own brand of pride.

"I have no comment," he told the press after we had met for
twenty minutes. "Nothing has changed." That meant I was still his
No. 1 heel. "This is a fine way for my players—or any players—to
treat me," he repeated. "He didn't tell me anything I didn't know before."

I told him the truth, which was the sole purpose behind my desire
to meet with him. He proceeded to make it obvious I was on the
team as a player but did not exist as a person. He would come to the
locker room and walk by me. It was a difficult situation, not only as
a player, but also because I was involved with his personal affairs.

I played up a storm that season. It might have been my best as a
Celtic. We beat Chamberlain, Thurmond, and the San Francisco

Warriors four games to one for another championship, but Walter Brown never said a word to me. He congratulated everyone else in the room, including the ballboys.

From our meeting after the All-Star game until the annual break-up dinner, he never nodded or even blinked an eye at me. The break-up dinner was a family affair with the wives at which the players would laugh and tell jokes on each other. Russell would arise and threaten to visit Ramsey for the summer so his southern friends could see who was coming to dinner.

Someone else invariably would tell about the card games and how much money Ramsey supposedly won or lost because he would hide such things from his wife. One season, the first year we won the championship, Ramsey lost over $200 in a card game but never informed Jean. He felt so guilty that during the summer, while out driving, he finally advised her he had something serious to tell her.

Jean Ramsey immediately thought there was another woman and she was going to be asked for a divorce. Frank did not realize it, but his marriage depended on what he was going to say. "I don't know how to tell you this," began Frank, as Jean became even more nervous. "I lost $238 playing cards during the playoffs in St. Louis."

She was relieved and graciously forgave her husband for having sinned that way. She had forgotten for the moment what money meant to him. All the wives, including Jean Ramsey, knew that Frank was the Jack Benny of pro basketball, and eventually they plotted against him.

The Celtic wives always shopped before a game at a woman's store called Morton's across from the Boston Garden. They would walk in with their packages and file into the row assigned to them behind our bench a few seconds before or after the game started. Frank would turn around to look for Jean and would become agitated if she had any packages. Spending was for other people.

One night the wives bought out the place. Missy Cousy, Lynn Loscutoff, Jean Ramsey, Ileana Sharman, and my wife decided to give Frank a shock. They learned something from their husbands.

They handed Jean Ramsey all the packages and she climbed into her seat loaded down. Frank, the little old lady of the Celtics, took his customary peek because he never wanted Red to see him looking over at the wives.

You should have seen the look on Frank's face when he spotted the packages. He waved frantically at his wife and gestured in a manner that made it obvious what he was trying to convey: "They're all ours? They're all ours?" He played terribly that night.

Those stories always brought a laugh at our break-up dinners no matter how often repeated. They may not sound funny to you but, remember, when you have just won a championship and the drinks are flowing, a reading of *Mein Kampf* would be humorous.

It finally got around to Walter Brown at the break-up dinner in the season of the eventful All-Star game. He made a brief talk. "We had a great season," he said. "I think that winning the championship could be attributed to only one player."

Bill Russell, naturally. We lost Cousy, Sharman, Ramsey, and even Heinsohn through the years, but the Celtics kept on winning as long as Russell was there to play. We all knew what Russ meant to the team, and everyone figured Walter Brown was going to congratulate him again.

"I attributed it all," he continued, "to a guy who worked tremendously hard for the ball club—Tommy Heinsohn." He sat down and I almost fell down. That was it. All over. He buried the hatchet just like that. He let it sink in by saying nothing else. I just sat and was tremendously touched that he had, in a sense, apologized publicly in his own way.

That summer I dropped into the office to resume business with him and he acted as though nothing had happened. That was the way he was in every respect. He would blow his horn and get it out of his system. He was the most accommodating and generous man I ever met.

I never made more than $28,500 a season as a player, excluding playoff money, but that was a lot in those days. For a long time, when Cousy was the main man, Walter Brown and Auerbach would never permit any Celtic to make more than Cooz. Even Russell could not be raised above Cousy, who, I believe, was one of the highest-paid players in the NBA at around $30,000 until Chamberlain came along to raise the standards way up high.

I remember once when Walter Brown and I went to the men's room and started negotiating. "What do you want?" he asked. I told him and, before we flushed the water, we had made a deal. Another time, they were painting the inside of the Garden, we walked upstairs, took one look, and by the time we got downstairs for a cab to take us to lunch, we had made an agreement.

It took Walter Brown five minutes to make a salary decision with a player. If Auerbach made a decision in five minutes, you knew he had gotten the better of you. Walter could never do that. He was father superior to all of us.

He was a popular man in Boston. He had a huge funeral, and I recall sitting in the third car from the end that was about a mile from the head of the cortege, which I could see because of a long dip in Route 9 on the way to Hopkinton.

He never got to sign the final papers for the estate on which I had worked. He would invite the players to his golf course at Oyster Harbors at the Cape, and I had talked to him about joining him over Labor Day so he could finalize his estate. "Don't bother coming down," he said. "I'll see you after the weekend. I'll be in the office on Tuesday and I'll sign the papers."

He died that weekend.

10

OUR PLANE DEVELOPED mechanical trouble so Auerbach decided to keep us overnight in Chicago. It was around one in the morning and taking a train to St. Louis, our next stop, was rejected as an unsound idea.

The NBA was partly a railroad league in those days, though planes were moving up fast and soon were to become the only means of travel. A problem arose. There weren't enough rooms for us to sleep two in a room.

That was resolved by placing cots in some rooms. Gene Conley and I were rooming together, and Cousy moved in for the night. It was the first time Conley had ever roomed with Cousy, and he was not aware of Bob's strange sleeping habits.

Conley was restless and decided to go for a few beers while Cousy and I went to bed because it was late and we were tired. Gene had been to Chicago many times during his baseball career, in which he had helped the Milwaukee Braves win a World Series, so he left to visit a favorite saloon while Cousy and I sacked out.

We received a wake-up call at six-thirty in the morning. I answered the phone, and Cousy and I started to dress when I noticed no one had slept in Conley's bed. Where the hell could he be? "I don't know," said Cousy. "I haven't the vaguest idea where he went."

I was first out of the room and headed for the lobby. We were supposed to leave at seven, and I intended to grab a quick cup of coffee. It was around ten minutes to seven when I reached the lobby and there was Conley, his suitcase alongside, sleeping on the couch.

I shook him and said: "Gino! Gino! Wake up!" He shook his head and sat up. "What the hell are you doing here, sleeping in the lobby?" I asked. "Cousy wouldn't let me in the room," he said.

I figured right away that Gene was suffering from too many beers. "What do you mean Cousy wouldn't let you in the room?" I asked. "He knew you were our roommate." Conley persisted. "He wouldn't let me in the room," he said once more.

I suggested he explain what had happened. "Well," he started, "I left my bag in the lobby, went out and had a couple of quick beers, came back, got my bag, and went upstairs to the room." So far, he made sense.

"I opened the door to the room," he continued, "and all of a sudden Cousy sat up in bed and said: 'Hey, you! Get out of the room and don't come back!' I thought he was kidding."

Then what? "I started for my bed," said Conley, "and he yelled: 'Hey, you! Get out of the room! Get out! Get out!' So I got out." Naturally, Gene wanted to know what the hell kind of guy was Cousy. I told him Cooz had some nerve doing that. After all, Conley was my roomie and Bob was only an emergency guest for the night.

When I saw Cousy, I informed him Conley had slept on the couch in the lobby and asked him to explain why he had chased Gene. "I didn't chase him," he insisted. "He just told me you threw him out when he came in last night," I informed him.

Cousy seemed mystified and then there was enlightenment. "Gee," he said. "I must've had another nightmare. I did dream last night that someone was chasing me." Conley never believed it. He thought Cousy didn't like him.

Conley was in no position to know that Cousy had been to doctors about nightmares. Sometimes he walked in his sleep. Sometimes he talked in his sleep. I think they told him it came from being too active and intense. He became so wound up by ball game activities, he would have nightmares.

One night he was rooming with Ramsey, and Frank rolled over in bed and sensed someone staring at him. He had an uneasy feeling. He opened his eyes and there was Cousy, sitting on the edge of the bed, looking at his throat.

Ramsey went to Auerbach the next day. "Look, Red," he said, "I know Cooz is a helluva guy, but I don't trust him when he's sleeping." I don't really know if Ramsey said it exactly that way, because sometimes he stuttered. We had a practice of appointing navigators when we were driving the maze of freeways out in Los Angeles, and Ramsey lost the job permanently because we would be beyond the exit before he could say Figuero or Fairfax.

Much has been written about the family attitude on the Celtics, and it was true. There never were cliques and, despite Auerbach's contribution to the smooth relationships, the players, themselves, had much to do with it. Cousy, as an individual, could be difficult to tolerate at times because he was a demanding person, but he subjugated himself like everybody where the team was concerned.

I was closer to Cousy than anyone because we lived in Worcester and had loyal Holy Cross ties. We would drive to practices together and enjoy practical jokes together. That still didn't prevent him from treating me with the same impatience as the others. His favorite trick at the start of a game was to deliberately overthrow two or three times to make you stretch out. It was his way of getting you primed for the fast break he ran.

After tossing the ball over the end line, he would grumble as though it had been your fault. He'd mumble something like: "Zudersumbdunadun." Something you couldn't possibly understand. Consequently, I called him Mr. Razzlefraz after the character in the Scripto television commercial who would grumble incoherently because he couldn't get his golf ball out of a trap.

We knew Cousy would throw too long deliberately but never questioned him. We knew he had great control of his passes and could peg the ball through a rubber tire from fifty feet away if necessary. He was like Tom Seaver tossing a knockdown pitch to get his message across.

Once, in Philadelphia, where the fans were as gentle as those in the Roman Colosseum in the days of Caesar, a teammate, Jack Nichols, solicited Cousy's aid. In those days, the games were played in Convention Hall, where the people were not as close to the playing surface as in Syracuse, Minneapolis, or some other cities.

Most of the crowd sat in a balcony that overlooked the court. There were seats on the floor but, because there was so much room, they were well removed from the sidelines and endlines. The players were within harassing distance, anyway.

For some reason, the best hecklers seemed to mobilize under the baskets. The favorite spot was near the visitors' bench. There sat the Nuremberg jury, a vocal group without music, and then there were the comedians, who preferred to work alone.

A Philadelphia comic tried out his act on Earl Strom one night in the Palestra, where a playoff game with the Knicks had been shifted because there was a circus in Convention Hall. There was a disturbance, and the referee called for the cops to remove the fan. "He kicked me," explained Earl, "so I kicked him back." That's what happens when you see too many Leo Durocher pictures.

There was another superb customer whose sole purpose for paying was to take out his hostilities on a player of his choice. It was remarkable the way he could maintain a constant flow of choice words without taking a deep breath. That went on for an entire game, and it would become annoying.

His favorite target for a while was Nichols, our resident dentist, who now practices in Seattle. "It's bad enough he is berating me with such horrible language," said Jack, "but he's got two kids with him. He's swearing all the time, which is no way for an adult to act in front of children."

Nichols and Cousy worked out a solution at half time. During the warmup, Nichols would take the ball off the basket, heave it out to Cousy, and then take a return pass. Jack, in the meantime, would stake himself out in front of the obnoxious fan, who was impairing the morals of minors with his foul words.

Cousy fired a bullet, Nichols stepped aside, and the ball hit the fan right in the stomach like a dumdum. He was a big, fat guy and the impact knocked him back into his seat. Though his wind was knocked out, the guy never missed a syllable and continued his abuse.

Nichols was enraged even more, so he picked up the ball and dribbled it off the fan's head. The fan understood that and never showed at another game, unless he shifted to an inconspicuous seat without our knowledge.

There was another conspicuous fan on the sidelines who derived great delight from irritating me. He was immense, weighing nearly three hundred pounds. He showed up with two beautiful girls for the season and always switched to new ones the next season. Crazy bookends.

I don't know why he was attracted to me when he had such nice company. Maybe I once smiled at him, which, some might insist, was the only time I ever smiled. He took a liking to me and would yell such things as: "Heinsohn, I saw you on television last week and you're destined for the Emmy." Not funny, but you know the type. One at every game.

I never became upset, but it was incessant and bothersome. It went on for a number of years, and I ignored him. I wouldn't give him the pleasure of responding. I would look over only to see the girls he was wearing on each arm.

One night, I noticed an unusual sight. The zipper on his pants was unzipped. "Now," I said to myself, "I will get even with this guy for playing to the crowd for laughs at my expense."

I put on my best scowl and took two steps in his direction while he was ranting about me and the crowd quieted, sensing something dramatic. "Now, pal," I said in a stage whisper that could be heard throughout the place, "I've been listening to you for five years. But there's no way I'm going to listen to you tonight."

That startled him. It might have even pleased him because he finally had been acknowledged. "Why?" he asked, meekly. I sucked in my stomach, thrust out my chest, and in great dramatic voice said: "I don't listen to guys who have their flies open." He dove for cover while I turned to the crowd and said: "Thank you very much."

The people broke up. Applause. He never came back after that. Too bad because they were such beautiful girls. We were fortunate the 76ers never complained that we were chasing their cash customers. As long as we had Russell and Cousy, the NBA didn't have to worry about losing attendance, anyway.

If I were to start a team, I would take Russell first and then Cousy because he made things happen. I played in a game with Cousy when Russell was hurt and we scored 173 points against the Lakers in the Boston Garden. With the 24-second clock.

Cousy was an explosive player but I believe a shy man underneath it all. He would sometimes have to psych himself to prepare for the intensity with which he played. For his final game, the 1963 championship series that ended in Los Angeles, he locked himself in his room for two days to get ready.

We were leading, three games to two, and the series could have gone to a seventh game back in Boston, but that meant nothing to Cousy. As far as he was concerned, the sixth game might be the decisive one, so he had his meals sent to his room and saw nobody. He isolated himself from the outside world and concentrated on the game. It was his form of transcendental meditation.

I considered myself a relatively calm individual, but there were times I would get nervous about a game. Russell would throw up. Auerbach would throw up, but sometimes I wondered if it was because of the Chinese food he consumed rather than the pressure. Once, I went to his apartment and actually saw hundreds of small, plastic containers filled with soy sauce on a mantelpiece. Red collected soy sauce like some people collected Ming vases, sculpture, or my paintings.

I had a friend in Los Angeles who worked for Douglas Aircraft, and he invited me to see the spacecraft being built. I asked Cousy to go, and he thought I was crazy indulging in such distractions at the time of a championship game. We beat the Lakers, 112–109, in the final game and sent Cousy back to normal, civilian life with a fifth straight title.

He wanted to go out the right way. He had been driven by fear of failure all the time, much like Russell. That's what made them such fierce competitors and winners. They were propelled by emotions that were concentrated and controlled deep inside them.

Except, of course, when Cousy was given a day on March 17, 1963, in Boston Garden after he had announced it would be his last season. He cried. Missy Cousy cried. Marie Collette and Mary Patricia, his daughters, cried. Red Auerbach cried. Adolph Schayes cried.

"I knew we were in trouble," one of the Syracuse players said after we won, 125–116, "when I saw the referees crying too." It was that kind of emotional affair. There hadn't been so much water since the Johnstown Flood.

That was the day I picked to score my ten thousandth point, of course. Nobody knew it. I never even received my basketball, a ritual every player experienced when something like that was accomplished.

Cousy was a sentimental and sensitive individual. I had seen him cry before. In my second year, we lost the final series to the St. Louis Hawks with Russell injured, and when we reached the locker room, Cousy broke down. He was the veteran and I was just out of my rookie shorts and all I did was grab another beer and sit on the floor. We lost the thing. So what? There'd be more.

It was important to me but there would be another season. Not for Cousy. He played like every game and season were his last. So I was not surprised when Bob Cousy Day became the most emotional scene in all my years with the Celtics.

Bill Sharman had retired two years before and was given nothing. I eventually retired in complete silence. Russell left quietly. I guess after Cousy got through, there were no more tears to shed.

It was St. Patrick's Day in Boston and they honored Cousy, the Frenchman. He attempted to speak a few times but kept breaking down. One of his daughters handed him her handkerchief and the family cried together.

I had heard stories of Lou Gehrig Day and Babe Ruth Day at Yankee Stadium and the hush that hung over those crowds. I'll tell you, Bob Cousy Day was a sequel when you consider that everyone knew Ruth and Gehrig were dying, while Cousy only was retiring.

All the Celtics had lumps in their throats. Even Russell's eyes glistened. I made up my mind I would never go through anything like that. I was offered a "day" before I quit but turned it down. I wanted to remember the Celtics for the laughs, not the tears.

That's the way I remembered Cousy. For the times he deliberately grabbed an extra cup of coffee at home when he was plotting with Ramsey to delay me so I would be fined for being late. For the time I was driving with him to an exhibiton game and we passed Auerbach on the road. We drove out of view, pulled over, and waited.

"What's wrong?" asked Red when he caught up with us. "We're out of gas," he was told. He chewed us out for being so dumb and went searching for gas in the Maine wilderness.

He was back around a half hour later with a couple of gallons. As he began removing them from his car, Cousy started our car and left Red standing there with his can in his hand. I preferred to remember Cousy that way rather than standing in front of 13,909 people sobbing his farewell.

It was moving, to be sure. I looked at Russell, who really wasn't that close to Cousy, and he was affected. Russ was truly gracious on that day—closer to Cousy than he had been in their six years as teammates.

These were the headlines of the day: "Cousy Weeps as 13,909 Roar Tumultuous Ovation" . . . "What Cousy Said—Amid Sobs— on Television" . . . "Hub's Tears Stir Cousy" . . . "Tearful Adieu to City's Best-loved Star" . . . "Tears Not out of Place at Farewell" . . . "Cousy Falters for First Time."

Nobody cried at my farewell but me. In fact, it is curious how quickly you are forgotten. That old gang of ours began breaking up when Sharman left, then Cousy and Ramsey, then me. Each year Russell and the others had to prove they were capable of winning without the missing Celtics.

I went through it when Cousy retired and Boston people assumed the NBA championships went with him. Russell probably suffered the most in that respect. Boston always considered him an intruder as long as Cousy was around to excite the people.

Let me recall some column excerpts of Tom Carey, a fine gentleman who, at first, did not recognize Russell's talent—for which he had all of Boston as company. "Is Russell worth seventeen thousand dollars?" he wrote shortly after Russ joined the Celtics. "No, because I can name three or four rebounders in the league that Russell fears."

Another time, partly motivated by Russell's autograph habits and desire to be left alone, Carey wrote: "In plain basketball sense, he is a vastly overpaid competitor. He has his ailments, also. Too tired to play more than twenty-four or twenty-five minutes per ball game. In the assist department, William pays little attention to where that ball is."

"Time to mention," he wrote in another column, "that Russell owes a great deal of his rebounding to Heinsohn. The ex-Holy Cross star is forever blocking out, which automatically forces Russell into a rebounding position." Eventually Tom Carey admitted he had been mistaken about Russell and publicly apologized, which made him a bigger man in my mind.

I think everyone in Boston finally was convinced about Russell when the Celtics won the 1964 championship without Cousy. I think we all dedicated ourselves to winning without him to prove ourselves. We won fifty-nine games—one short of our own NBA record.

We destroyed the Cincinnati Royals with Jerry Lucas, Oscar Robertson, and Wayne Embry, four games to one, in the Eastern Conference final.

Our last stop on the way to a sixth straight title was the San Francisco Warriors with Wilt Chamberlain, Nate Thurmond, and Al Attles; Al was to get his first championship ring many years later when he coached the Golden State Warriors to the 1975 title against Washington.

The way we won the final game, 105–99, to take the series, four games to one, was symbolic in many ways. I made a critical play against Chamberlain when it was a two-point game in the closing seconds, but it was Russell who was acclaimed for putting in a wide-open rebound. What else was new?

I was always considered a playoff player by those close to the club. My pleasure came from improvising anything that would help us win, yet, at times, people never recognized it. They laughed, for example, when I told them what I had done to enable Russell to score off my rebound when it was 101–99.

First, here was how they recorded the play in the newspapers: "It was Bill Russell who jammed home the vital 103rd point on a two-hand rebound when he eluded the great Wilt Chamberlain to tally after Tommy Heinsohn missed a close-in shot." Eluded Chamberlain?

Now what really happened. They set me up for the last shot. Thurmond was guarding me and I was to drive on him. I got by Nate as planned, and Chamberlain dropped off Russell to harass me. I was surrounded by seven-footers. I couldn't see the basket, Russell, or anything. I was a poor little chipmunk lost in a forest.

What the hell was I to do with the ball? I had to shoot it left-handed, but I couldn't shoot because of the tall trees all around. I realized Russell would be coming off the other side, so all I tried to do was put it off the board as softly as possible. Actually, I passed it off the backboard. Don't laugh.

Russ took it off the right side and jammed it. After the game, everyone was wild about the great stuff shot Russell had just made to clinch the championship. Walter Brown came over and asked what happened on the play and I told him I had passed the ball to Russell off the backboard.

People got hysterical. I was serious, but it was treated as the biggest joke in a locker room full of joking. Amid it all, K. C. Jones turned to Ramsey and Loscutoff, playing their final game, and said: "Maybe it sounds funny because I'm black and you're white but the Celtics are a family. I'll feel your losses deeply."

I wondered how Chamberlain felt that night. He had played well but lost again. By then the idea of Russell winning so much had to be getting to Wilt. The only pleasurable thing Wilt took out of the series was the knowledge he finally had gotten even with Clyde Lovellette for breaking his jaw.

Lovellette was with us at the time, but a few years earlier with St. Louis, he had smashed Wilt's jaw with one of his educated elbows. Clyde was cute that way. He would knock you down, pick you up, dust you off, and say "Gee," as though he was sorry about the accident.

My favorite recollection was the way he'd talk to a man dribbling around the foul area. He would say: "Glad to see you. Did you have a good summer? How's the wife and kids? I heard you have a radio show." Then you would take a foul shot and he'd rap you right in the mouth. The original Mr. Nice.

It was not difficult to understand why people didn't like Clyde, though he had a sense of humor that was funny sometimes. For instance, the time he had a terrible experience with the officiating of the late Jim Duffy, who threw him out of a game. They argued and Clyde threatened to get Duffy at the first opportunity.

Duffy had no idea as to whether Lovellette was kidding or what he had in mind. Jim went out after the game to drink a lot and eat a little, and he returned to his room with a nice glow. Meanwhile, Lovellette, a member of the Quick Draw Club, had gone to his room and strapped on the six-shooters he carried with him all the time.

Duffy was just climbing into bed when there was a knock on the door. He opened it and there stood Lovellette with his guns full of blanks. Clyde yanked them both and said: "I've got you now!" and fired. Duffy took a nose dive under the bed.

Wilt shot up Lovellette pretty good in the second game of our series with the Warriors on our court. Wilt had restrained himself from hitting anyone in the league until that time but had made a vow to deck Clyde for making him take liquid food through a wired jaw. We were in the fourth period of a 124–101 victory when they called a foul on Lovellette for shoving Wilt, and then it happened.

Clyde was insulted. Wilt was insulted because Clyde was insulted. They traded insults and then Wilt let him have one in the mouth. Clyde stood there transfixed, quivered for a few seconds, and sank slowly to his knees, blood streaming. One punch was Wilt's revenge.

Sam Jones had come close to being Wilt's first victim two seasons earlier, when Chamberlain was with Philadelphia. That's when Sam improvised and grabbed a stool in self-defense against the monstrous Warrior. "I wasn't going to fight him fair—I was going to have a chair," explained Sam, a fistic poet long before Muhammad Ali.

And why not? Wilt had speared him in the chest in the fifth game of the 1962 playoff series with Philadelphia and then came at him with his hand extended. Chamberlain claimed he intended to shake hands to show he was sorry, but Sam thought otherwise. "He had been jawing at me," said Sam, "and when he moved his hands toward me, I wasn't taking any chances."

Sam grabbed a photographers' stool from the end line and prepared for the big tiger's attack. I guess Sam suddenly remembered how often he had taunted Wilt when we ran the fast break at him. Wilt would drop back to protect the middle and then move out to block the shot. Sam would shoot his jumper just high enough to teasingly graze Wilt's fingertips and yell: "Too late, Wilt!"

My roommate got the worst of it, though. Carl Braun was standing with Guy Rodgers and saying he would get the stool from Sam, but then Guy hit Carl in the eye with a sneak punch. I didn't like Guy and Loscutoff didn't like Guy and, when he saw that, we went for the guy.

Rodgers took off and we chased him all around the Boston Garden. Loscutoff got his hand on him once but Guy slipped away like a greased pig. We played tag up the court, around the court, and across the middle, and Rodgers finally escaped through an exit. It was the greatest broken-field run in basketball history.

Braun never had a chance of catching Guy on his own that night or in the remaining games of the series we won, four games to three, because he had no playing time. Carl was only a sub playing out his last season after the Knicks had fired him as coach. He wouldn't let me forget what Rodgers had done to him.

Carl retired and became a stockbroker in New York over the

summer but made a special trip to Boston for our first game with the Warriors the next season. "Hawk," he said, "you gotta get Guy Rodgers for me." I explained that was last season. "You're not gonna let an old roomie down, are you?" he said. "But Carl," I said "I can't even catch the guy." And I never did.

11

I WAS MAD at Auerbach. He knew I was quitting after the 1964–65 season, yet he let me finish my career on the bench while the Celtics were beating the Lakers, 129–96, for the championship they had dedicated to the memory of Walter Brown.

It was heartbreaking for me to watch Willie Naulls playing in my position and the Celtics putting away their seventh straight title without me. I was terribly hurt, my wife was terribly hurt, my mother and father were terribly hurt, the entire Heinsohn clan was terribly hurt.

I had informed Red two weeks before the draft and before the playoffs that I planned to retire, so he could seek a replacement. The fun had gone out of it for me. The traveling, the whirlpool treatments, the pushing of my tired body and mind made me too nervous and unhappy.

I had missed five weeks when I developed a blood clot after tearing something between my big toe and heel in December and had struggled in discomfort all season. The Celtics won eighteen in a row without me, and there were other things that convinced me they could get along without me very well. Actually, I felt left out and not needed.

I had fought the inner struggle all season until my insurance company told me there was an agency available if I wanted it. Everything came together right then. I couldn't play in the All-Star game because I was hurt, the Celtics were going on without me, and the business opportunity made up my mind that I should hang up my basketball shoes, as they call them now.

I went to Red in his office and said: "I don't know what you're thinking, but I'm planning on quitting. I think I'm gonna quit." He didn't believe me and suggested I think it over. I assured him I had done that, so by the time we had taken a lead of three games to one over the Lakers with Jerry West, Dick Barnett, and Don Nelson, he knew that the fifth game would be my last if we won.

We blew it open in the third period and Red removed Russell with 5:51 to go and then the other starters, but I still sat on the bench. The fans chanted: "We want Heinsohn! We want Heinsohn!" but I sat. I had come out in the third period and never went back, convincing me I was absolutely right when I had concluded I wasn't a necessary part of the Celtics anymore.

There had been a flickering hope deep inside that I might change my mind about quitting until that happened. They didn't need me, they could win without me and didn't think I was important to them anymore. And, truthfully, I wasn't. It was my time to follow Sharman and Cousy to the dressing room in the sky.

I had played as hard as I could for the Celtics, and I wanted to leave with dignity. I didn't want to feel I was cheating anyone, especially myself. That did not ease the pain of having Red let me sit while time ran out on me. With a minute to go, when it was all over, he asked: "Do you want to go back in?" and I told him: "No, I don't want to go back in."

He missed the point. I wanted to be part of it, and the last minute was not part of it for Tommy Heinsohn. I didn't want to be an afterthought. Later I was to better understand Red's thinking and realize only my pride was hurt, and sometimes that can distort things. But then, I was awfully upset and tears came to my eyes as it ended with me on the bench and people asking: "Why didn't he put you in?"

Auerbach, not insensitive, sensed something was wrong and invited me to sit alongside him in the lead car the next day in the championship motorcade through Boston. He never knew how destroyed I had been when Diane and I went out after the game with the Loscutoffs. Jim had retired the year before and had gone through the same disturbing finish on the bench. Diane and I had consoled him on his night, the Loscutoffs consoled me on my night. Big men playing little boys' games.

We wound up agreeing that Auerbach had other players who also had feelings that deserved to be considered. When I had the chance to look at it from an unselfish viewpoint, I concluded I wouldn't have put Tommy Heinsohn back in the game, either. Big deal.

I know people think of Tommy Heinsohn in terms of the terrible temper, the fights, the angry faces, and the animal disposition, but underneath is a person as sensitive and prone to life's problems as anyone. I too had to search for answers when, for example, my youngest son, David, began showing signs of a serious health complication at an early age.

I was Tommy Heinsohn, No. 15 on the championship Celtics, but I was father and husband to a family. It is difficult to describe the pressure of trying to entertain people and yourself while your wife is at home facing the complexities of a son showing symptoms of retardation when he was five. Eventually we discovered that David suffered from dyslexia, a not uncommon hearing disfunction that also had afflicted Vice President Rockefeller when he was ten.

While I was playing for the Celtics, and into my coaching years, Diane had the full responsibility of taking David to the doctors, psychiatrist, hospital, and then The School for Special Learning, which finally straightened him out. How much more difficult and less stimulating that was for Diane and David than leaving home everyday to play basketball for fun, fame, money, and the Celtics.

I was able, at least, to forget the constant family pressures while playing ball. Diane had to live with them every moment. In fact, life had been a little cruel to David since he was around eighteen months old.

That's when we first noticed he was stumbling and then that his knees were crooked. He had to be placed in full leg braces for almost two years. I remember that we took him, Paul, and Donna to the Ice Show at the Boston Garden and I couldn't carry him because I had been hurt and the braces were so heavy.

Diane, of course, lifted David and began carrying him to our seats up two steep flights of stairs. An usher I knew saw that and grabbed David and immediately reacted to the weight of the braces. That was an extra load for Diane.

The worst began developing when we detected signs of David having reading problems in the first grade. Tests showed he was not slow mentally, but we were concerned about the symptoms. In back of our minds, like all parents, was the possibility of brain damage that might be coming to the surface.

We remembered when he was two and three and would doze off anytime something happened to him. If he hurt his finger and we applied a Band-Aid, he would fall asleep in the process. If we took him to the dentist, he would fall asleep in the chair so that a block of wood had to be placed between his teeth to keep his mouth open.

All those things were happening while I was away with the Celtics winning championships in 1962, 1963, and 1964. Somewhere along the way, it was detected that David had suffered a hearing loss, but he kept going to public schools while being tutored three times a week to keep him from falling too far behind.

In the fifth grade, his teacher informed Diane that David was keeping up with the children only through special attention but not in open class and, since the next year two teachers would be handling sixty-two pupils, she suggested a change. They would not have the time David needed. On top of that, he had developed insecurities because of what he had been going through.

The children would see him going for special tutoring and taunt him. They'd call him a dummy, and he became thoroughly convinced he was a dummy.

He was a boy of ten speaking the language of a seven-year-old. His hearing distortion had made it difficult to pick up words in open class. Also, he had grown terribly insecure, so he used the simplest words that came to mind. He was going deeper into a shell.

I'd take the three kids to the Boston Garden for a game, and someone always wanted a family picture. Donna and Paul would fight to be in front near their daddy, who was the Celtic coach by then. David hid himself along my leg or behind me.

One night I sat with Diane and went over the entire situation. The idea was to try to determine what was best for David, who deserved a lot better than his mother and father had been able to provide.

That's when we decided on mental therapy. Diane drove David to Boston once a week for two years, mainly because I was away so much. David would see the psychiatrist, and Diane would consult with a social worker, who tuned her in to how to handle her son. All three worked separately, but it was connected. They called it a triangle.

Today, I am thankful to say, David is an outgoing, popular young man after five years of drifting from everything we considered normal. I am prouder of what he accomplished than anything I have ever done or anyone in the family has done. I remember how proud I was of Donna, the oldest, as I watched her go from the bunnies to the rabbits to the puppy dogs in her dance recitals. I am proud of how Paul has developed into an athlete with healthy interests.

David was exceptional because he had to fight and struggle for so long. He had to overcome. It is an indescribable feeling when you see your son, despite the hardships, play the piano or express his feelings and sensitivity on canvas. It can make a big brute cry—and it did.

I learned a lot from David, Donna, Paul, and Diane, and I can only hope they learned something from me, as I did my best not to be an absentee father. I know there was a time when they had to have inordinate patience as the old man of the family suffered withdrawal pains after I had quit playing.

It had seemed so simple after I had made the decision. The headlines told the story better than I could: "Weep Not for Heinsohn: He Has a $20,000 Job" . . . "Tom Heinsohn Joins Wagner Agency" . . . "Heinsohn Always Came up with Tricky Shots" . . . "Heinsohn Greatest in the Clutch" . . . "Tom Feels Sad Leaving Celts" . . . "Heinsohn Retires, Placed on Farm List." Just like that it was over.

I never could understand how there could be such a high when we won a championship and then absolute low a few days later. One day the whole world is full of bubbles and excitement, and then as though it had been all a dream. That's the feeling that grew and grew inside of me as I moved deeper into retirement and the business future I had chosen.

I had started playing in the sixth grade when I was twelve, but now was only thirty, so people concluded I still had a lot of basketball left in me. "Don't quit," I was advised by fans and friends. Diane left the decision to me because I had left it to her when her time came to decide between basketball and me.

Diane had been a player, coach, and referee. You can't imagine me living in the same house with a referee? It could've been worse. It could've been Richie Powers. I really shouldn't say that because I still feel badly about what I once did to him. I think I forced him to retire once.

I played exactly eighteen minutes in a game against Los Angeles in 1965 because Powers fouled me out. Earl Strom made four calls that Richie reversed. I flipped, and Auerback flipped, in that order. Powers got so mad, he flung his whistle at Red.

I was a big moaner and griper and, I guess, I forced Powers to lose his poise and erupt to the point where he said after that game that he no longer could tolerate NBA basketball. He was so distraught, he quit when the season ended. He returned, of course, and I want him to know how sorry I am for what I did to him. I am not seeking favors, but anything he can do for the Celtics would be appreciated.

I did plead for sympathy once with Sid Borgia, who apparently learned how to referee from his Aunt Lucretia, also well known at one time. Sid was the originator of the no-harm, no-foul interpretation, which boosted Blue Cross sales in the league but did little for foul shooting or the sanity of the players.

I worked out a campaign for Borgia. I tried reasoning. I tried getting mad, which was not easy for me, obviously. Then I tried total indifference. I still reached the line once or twice a game if I was lucky.

I finally decided on humor, my strong point. I realized that seemed impractical because it was easier to make the faces on Mount Rushmore smile than Borgia. But it was my last resort.

So one day we played on national television and I hadn't gone to the line by the fourth quarter. "Look, Sid," I said, finally, "it's the fourth quarter and my mother hasn't seen me in six months." That reached him. "Whaddya mean your mother hasn't seen you in six months?" he asked. "What's that got to do with me?" I had my opening.

"My mother hasn't seen me in six months," I repeated, "and if you get me to the foul line, there'll be a nice, big closeup of me on television. My mother, who lives in New Jersey, will be able to see I'm okay, and she'll be happy."

Sid chuckled as we went up the floor. My man was about two feet away but Sid blew the whistle and called a foul. I stepped to the line and, as he flipped the ball, he said: "That's it for your mother." He never gave me another foul shot for the next five games.

Fortunately, Diane didn't walk around the house in a striped shirt and with a whistle in her mouth. Her active involvement in basketball ended when we got married. I simply did not want to come home and find a wife out somewhere playing basketball, as happened when I was at Holy Cross.

One weekend I traveled all the way from Worcester to New Jersey to see her and she was in a tournament in Newburgh, New York. She was good, though. We used to go to Lake Hopatcong with another couple and play two-on-two. The Heinsohns were the mixed doubles champions of the world in those days.

Diane handled her own retirement story and I had to handle mine. I was deeply involved in the insurance agency after I quit, but I also went to a lot of games. I went with clients to enjoy the action and, if the Celtics lost, people would come to me and say: "Boy, they would've won it if you were in there."

I smiled at the recognition, but it meant nothing. I was there to forget, yet things kept happening to prevent that. The Celtics had trouble at the start of the 1965–66 season. Don Nelson, picked up from the Lakers, on my recommendation as my replacement because he had been so tough on me, was having trouble breaking in. Willie Naulls was beginning to lose it.

Auerbach came to me one night and told me it was the toughest year he ever had to coach. It was wearing him out. I was far removed from that and didn't miss it. I had made the tough transition. I had mastered the agony of retirement. I had lived through the toughest part, the first year, and was on my way.

I had sat down with many players after they had retired and told them not to worry about the first year. They'd be so happy. The day

I quit, I had made a promise I never would put on another pair of basketball shoes and run. I figured I must have run around the world a dozen times on the fast break alone.

I eagerly looked forward to not ever running again. I was able to walk in a normal pair of shoes and at a normal pace in my insurance business. I had no idea what normal living was until I was out of basketball for one year. When I found out, I hated it.

In my second year, the withdrawal symptoms began showing. That's when I discovered I had been so conditioned by basketball, I could not adjust to the insurance business, as much as I liked it. I had become accustomed to immediate results—in forty-eight minutes I either won or lost. In insurance, I had to wait six months for this guy to make up his mind or four months for that guy.

I also found out that Tommy Heinsohn, strictly the insurance agent, was treated differently. It no longer was: "Hey, baby. How's the ball club?" I was plain Tommy Heinsohn, no longer associated with the Celtics. I hadn't realized how important the sports identity had been to me.

I had been something special since I was twelve, when my mother would delay dinner until I finished playing basketball in the schoolyard. I had been set apart for eighteen years and been given special treatment. Now if I was late for dinner, I was late for dinner. People went on without me. Life seemed to go on without me.

The relationship with the family became different and difficult because of me. I began eating breakfast, lunch, and dinner at home with Diane and the kids. I wasn't used to them, they weren't used to me. There had never been a nine-to-five routine in our house. My family had never seen me come home at five o'clock, take my shoes off, put on my slippers, and sip a beer.

I was a stranger in my own home. I could find no special reason for anyone to cater to my whims. All my life I had been accustomed to everyone making concessions because I was Tommy Heinsohn, the tired ballplayer, who wanted to eat when he desired or wanted to sleep when he desired or wanted to go someplace when he desired.

I had taken all those things for granted until I was out of basketball a year and then realized I no longer deserved to be catered to if anyone really cared anymore. It was so abnormal, I didn't know

when to argue or not to argue with Diane. I was out of synchroniza-
tion—or "sync," as they say in television and the movies. I had
walked so many years down the other road that the one leading to a
normal family adjustment was full of holes and ditches for me.

My insurance job got on my nerves. I had enjoyed the freedom
of traveling around the country and world, so my office seemed like
the tiger cages of Vietnam. I found myself engaging in such exciting
activities as tracking down paper clips or turning the air conditioning
on and off.

God help me when it rained. I had to get out of the office and
pace the hallway or go to lunch for two hours. I had become deeply
disturbed because I wasn't being me. I was like the movie star, the
sex symbol, who suddenly discovered she had wrinkles where a sex
kitten shouldn't have wrinkles.

I am sure Diane preferred seeing the garbageman or the mail-
man in those days. I represented a lot more pressure on top of the
normal pressures of running a household with three growing children with faster-growing appetites. I had a problem that was
screaming inside my head and stomach.

I was confused for the first time in my life. Answers had been
supplied me so often, I didn't know the answers to my own urgent
questions. I was born all over, again, in that respect.

It was like a man of sixty-five being forced to retire before his
time and then proceeding to dry up and die. I had to develop a new
way of life at a young age, and that was bewildering. I had a career
all set up in insurance management, and suddenly I was saying:
"Hey, where the hell am I?"

I caused confusion at home and all around because I was struggling for meanings. I had been successful in everything I had ever
done, but I had anxieties and feelings of insecurity. I wanted to talk
to someone—anyone. Help me! Someone help me!

I talked to many people. I spoke with Missy Cousy. She sent me
to see a priest at Holy Cross, a friend. He sent me to someone else.
Nothing. Then one night I went to a party Bill Russell threw for
K. C. Jones, who was retiring that season, which was 1966–67.

At the party was John Mallon, someone I had known for years.
He lived in Framingham and was very close to K.C. Somehow he
had heard about the problems I was having. "I'm going to give you

the name of someone to talk to," he said. "You know him. He's Father Joe Shea. He's the head of the Philosophy Department at Holy Cross."

I told Mallon I wasn't going to see Father Shea because I had no faith in him. I was confused enough. "Do yourself a favor," said Mallon. "Go see him. I did. I had some personal problems and he straightened my head out in ten minutes."

Mallon convinced me, and I called that Monday for an appointment. I walked into Father Shea's office the next day. "I'm not surprised to see you," he announced before I hardly had said hello. "Really, Father, why?" I responded.

He looked at me. "You never failed at anything, did you?" he said. "What do you mean, Father?" I said. "You're just totally successful," he said. "You've got to come to the realization that you are going to fail. You are going to fail."

We talked for an hour and half, and he made me finally recognize myself. I was a plugger. I was persistent and I had to do it the right way. I had created my own stresses and pressures and, in effect, I was afraid to make a mistake. I was afraid to admit I made a mistake to anyone but, more importantly, to myself.

Father Shea opened my eyes and mind. I had to do it right all the time. He made me realize: Why can't I make mistakes? Why did I have to tell myself I had to be right? So what if I made a mistake?

I had pursued the right way, my way, so stubbornly that I considered the other way the wrong way. Everyone but me was mistaken because I never made mistakes. I discovered I had made ten thousand mistakes. I discovered that even when I am trying hard, it might be the wrong way, so what's the difference? As long as you can say "Hey, baby. I didn't do it maliciously. I just did the wrong thing."

It came down to a love-hate thing. If I didn't like myself, I couldn't like anybody else. I actually had to learn how to like myself before I realized I had been too demanding and expected too much from everyone around me. Including me.

Fortunately, Father Shea and Uncle Red came to my rescue. Father Shea with his perceptive analysis, and Auerbach because once more he sensed I was disturbed and went out of his way to get me involved with the televising of Celtic games.

That was the season Auerbach decided to quit coaching and

concentrate on the business end of the organization. I might have been the first one in whom he confided the change. He had been running everything. He would get off a road trip and would be in the office at eight o'clock in the morning to handle the details before practice and games.

He loved to coach but I suspected it was becoming too much for him. I learned it was going to happen when I went to Philadelphia to buy some clothes early in the 1965–66 season and he asked me to have lunch with him.

"I'm gonna quit," he told me in late October or early November. "Are you interested in the job?" I was only a few months into my retirement and a long way from the major crisis in my life. "I'm happy in the insurance business," I said. "I want to give that a shot. I'm making an awful lot of money right now with the agency."

Then I mentioned another consideration—Russell. "I couldn't handle Russell," I said, candidly. "Russell would never play for me. I couldn't motivate him. The only guy who can handle him is you or himself."

I asked Red whom he had in mind. "You, Ramsey, Cousy," he replied. "I don't think Cousy would want it," I said. "He's coaching at Boston College. I don't think Ramsey could handle Russell, either. The only one who can get the most out of Russell is Russell. Why not make him the coach?"

I am sure I influenced Red to at least consider the critical fact that Russell would play harder for himself than for anyone else. Red went on to consider Bob Brannum and others but eventually came back to Russell. As it turned out, when I quit playing, I had a hand in picking Nelson as my successor because, as slow as he seemed, I never could drive around him. Then I had a hand, or mouth, in helping Red pick Russell as his successor. I guess I was entitled to a gold star for being so smart.

I was flattered that Red offered me the job first, though I could not take it. I remained in close touch with him as the season progressed. I would stop in the office and he would give me names of potential insurance clients. We kept the relationship going.

Russell ultimately was announced as the new coach just before the Celtics beat the Lakers in the seventh game for another championship. I am sure the timing was planned by Red as a motivating factor to balance the edge Jerry West, Elgin Baylor, and Rudy

LaRusso had by playing the final game at home. Another example of Auerbach's shrewdness.

It was shortly before the dramatic announcement that Russell would be replacing Red as coach that my television career began. Auerbach, as general manager, allowed only one home game to be televised during the final playoff, and that is when he arranged for me to handle the color. Little did I realize the price I would have to pay.

12

"H EY," SAID RED AUERBACH, during the summer of 1966, "we're going to be televising road games this season on Channel 56. Are you interested in doing the play-by-play?" I gulped. I had never minded going one-on-one with Chamberlain or Lovellette or Maurice Stokes, but doing play-by-play made me apprehensive.

"I've never done anything like that, Red," I said, skeptically. "Play-by-play is a tough job." He assured me I could do it and shouldn't worry about it. Once more I was being advised to belt Wilt because it wouldn't hurt Red.

He had the strategy all worked out, naturally. "What we'll do is get Marty Glickman and have him break you in," he said. "He'll train you for a few games. He's agreed to do it. Give it a shot." I was shaken but grateful because it was ideal therapy after my unfortunate experience earlier that year with withdrawal pains.

Marty broke me in for three or four games. I acquired the feel of the microphone, the pace of the game, the commercials, and the entire mechanics. I borrowed the Celtics' videotape equipment and practiced at home games. Fred Cusick, the sports director of Channel 56, would sit alongside and review my homework after the Boston Garden games.

I practiced as often as I could until they finally decided I was ready for Marty to leave me on my own. I had no color man, nothing. I did every commercial, every lead-in, and the halftime interview without a problem, which made me feel great—like the night I scored 47 points in Seattle. Only this time, a star was born in Baltimore.

I sweated frequently that first show but I drank enough Cokes to cool me off. That led to the discovery of an occupational hazard of TV announcers. It is called the relief stop by truck drivers and other patrons of the highways. It is called something more descriptive by ballplayers when they go to the dressing rooms at half time.

Anyway, I discovered that if you drank lots of liquids, and commercials ran about a minute and you were the sole announcer, there was no time left for other things. I was quite uncomfortable for a while until experience provided the answer, as it generally does. "Folks," I would say, "we're going to pause now for station identification."

Those turned out to be the longest station breaks in history. They had to keep it going until I ran to the men's room and got back to the mike—and I was never known for my speed even when I wasn't racing with a handicap. I think my only fluff the night of my first solo flight involved the lead-in to the Friday night movie: *Yankee Doodle Dandy.*

"Make sure you remain tuned in immediately following the ball game," I said, "for *Yenkel Doodle Dendy.*" Then I said: "Of course, that's a Jewish movie." I was proud of myself. Howard Cosell couldn't have ad-libbed like that—and probably wouldn't have.

Whenever I made mistakes, I would have more damn fun doing it. I had learned about mistakes, remember? Still, it was a tedious, difficult one-man job for an amateur Johnny Most. I kept telling the people at the station that they must send someone with me for at least half time. Help me. I had to at least go to the men's room. Triple spot the commercials because it was way up on the second floor.

That's how Boston's version of Huntley and Brinkley or the

Frick and Frack of the airways developed. Despite great expense, and with little concern for me, they gave me Auerbach as color man. He didn't do all the games, which indicated the people at the station had some compassion after all.

The new broadcasting team worked the games in Baltimore, Philadelphia, and New York, primarily. I did others by myself. If Thomas Edison had known his inventive mind might lead to Auerbach and Heinsohn on television, he would have gone into medicine.

Red loved peanuts almost as much as Chinese food and was forever eating them during the telecasts. We were working a playoff game in Philadelphia and he dropped the bag on the floor. As Red reached for the peanuts, Chet Walker drove toward the hoop and was leveled by Larry Siegfried.

Everyone in the arena and watching television at home had seen the play except Red. He had been involved with a more important matter. Walker was stretched out when Red finally looked to the court. "What's he doing?" he screamed into his mike. "Is he pulling that same old jazz about twenty seconds?"

Red was referring to the unlimited automatic times-out NBA players had been known to take and fake for one reason or another. Each team now is entitled to only one twenty-second "injury" time-out a half with no questions asked, and some players, such as Bill Russell and Walt Frazier, made a career out of the opportunity to rest.

"He's not hurt," Red told the home audience. "He wasn't even in on the play." I'm sure the viewers must have flipped the dials to see what game Red was watching. I knew he had made a mistake because of the peanuts and I had to say something to cover. "Red," I said, informatively, "He was driving toward the basket and Siegfried hit him."

A normal person wouldn't have touched that with a ten-foot pole, but Red was not one to give up that easily. He could take any side of a debate and argue vigorously—and convincingly. He had chosen to say Walker had not been in on the play, and everyone was stuck with that.

"He wasn't involved in the play," he said, brusquely. Now he had me on the hook. How do I get out of that one? It had become a battle of wills. A one-on-one confrontation, and I had the ball.

Walker was still on the floor, and the great television debate continued. "Siegfried knocked him down," I said, lowering my voice and hoping Red would take the hint. "He was not in the play!" insisted Red, his voice rising.

"Okay, Red," I finally said. "Have it your way. He was not in the play, but would you settle for this—he was in the movie?" I'll say this for Red—he had me thinking all the time as to how to escape his situations. He was totally undisciplined and uninhibited. He told it like it was—as long as it favored the Celtics. But it was fun and some times funny.

Red would do the halftime interviews. One time his guest was Eddie Gottlieb, a league pioneer as original owner of the Philadelphia franchise. Gotty had a habit of grabbing the microphone when it came time to speak. It never occurred or mattered to him that the mike was sensitive enough to pick up sounds a few feet away.

The first thing I learned when I wandered into televisionland was never give up the microphone. That weapon put you in command. Yielding it would be like shooting without the ball, which, come to think of it, I had been accused of at times.

Auerbach would ask a question and Gottlieb would yank the mike from him. They proceeded to have a beautiful tug-of-war as the interview progressed. I went to the men's room and, when I came back, there they were, two little kids battling over a toy. Unfortunately, the home audience never saw it. "Listen, you guys," I told them, finally. "This wrestling match is over. We've got to pause for a commercial."

I was a novice but I always made sure I didn't leave Red on the microphone too long—that is, until the Celtics went to Los Angeles for the sixth game of the 1967–68 championship, which they won, four games to two, in Russell's first season as player-coach.

By then I was a professional and had the responsibility of setting up everything. Red never concerned himself with technical aspects or preparations. He was completely spontaneous, which, as I have explained, could be a problem.

"If we win this game tonight," the director told me, "there'll be a championship celebration, so we better prepare for locker room interviews. If it looks as though the Celtics are going to win with a minute to go, have Red rush downstairs for the interviews while you wrap up."

That sounded fine. Red strolled in one minute before the start of the game, as usual. I repeated the director's instructions. "They've got a camera set up downstairs for interviews if we win it," I said. "It's a long ways down and it'll take about a minute for the players to reach the dressing room, so take off with a minute to play."

Red never hesitated. "You do it," he said. I explained there were a lot of commercials and other copy that had to be read for the wrapping up. "I'll do that," he volunteered. "You go down and start the interviews."

I tried to convince him the other way would be easier. I'm sure Mendy Rudolph was more convincing in his attempts to rationalize with Red. Since I couldn't hit him with two technicals and chase him, I said: "Okay."

Sure enough, the Celtics blew it open, winning, 124–106. John Havlicek played a superb game. He hit over 40 points and was just sensational. I suggested to the living room set that Havlicek had been outstanding in the whole series—simply super. "I wouldn't say that, Tom," said Red, unpredictably but predictably.

"You wouldn't say that?" I improvised for the occasion and the people in Boston. "What more could the man have done?" I was trying to be charitable. "Well," he said, "it wasn't only Havlicek." Granted. "I didn't mean to imply it was only Havlicek," I countered, apologetically. "I just thought he put on a stellar performance."

That took place near the end of the game. I wanted to leave the people at home with an appraisal of what Havlicek had contributed to another championship. As I prepared to leave for the locker room, I figured I had better smooth the way for Red's first experience at wrapping up a show. "As soon as they give you the cue," I told him, "flip the mike on and close the show. After the commercials, wrap it up and throw it to me in the locker room."

I left and headed down the back spiral stairway that led to the subterranean chambers of the Forum. We had the cameraman inside the Celtic room, and I waited outside for the players to arrive. The team came walking through the tunnel and went into the room, closing the door. I figured a minute or so and we would all be invited in.

Nope. The door opened and the cameraman came out, then the director came out. "What's the matter?" I asked. "Russell threw us out," they explained. "What for?" I asked. "He said they were going to have a meeting," they said.

"A meeting?" I replied. "After winning the championship? Did you tell him we must get in to send the interviews back to Boston? That Auerbach was upstairs filling time until I relieved him?" I was informed that Russell had been so informed but he had chased them, anyway.

I steamed. Then I laughed when I thought of Auerbach upstairs fumbling for words for the first time in his life. He filled and filled and filled as Russell kept us out five minutes, ten minutes, fifteen minutes. By then I was hysterical from laughing, of course. I had no way of telling what Red was saying because I was not plugged in, but I knew it had to be panic time for the old redhead.

Russell opened the door after fifteen minutes, which could be a lifetime to anyone who had never filled that much air time. I got into the dressing room and found out that the delay had been caused by a prayer meeting and discussions of togetherness, Celtic pride, and all such things. I put the microphone in front of Russell and then Havlicek, which is when Auerbach showed up.

Red should have been grinning from hair strand to hair strand, or at least smoking a championship cigar, but he glared at me as though I had just done him a great evil or asked for the address of the State Department woman who once bought him the alligator bag. "Here's Red Auerbach," I said as I handed him the mike for the remaining interviews. "Wasn't it terrific?"

I moved away before he had a chance to tell me how terrific it had been. I don't think the television tubes or the FCC could have tolerated what he was prepared to call me—for no good reason.

I still had no idea as to what Red had said to consume fifteen minutes. I'm sure his bar mitzvah speech had taken less time. I wasn't about to ask Red, so I waited until we returned to Boston and then hustled to the studio. I arranged to have them show me those closing minutes from the Wonderful World of Red Auerbach.

"Well, now," said Red on the videotape. "It was a great victory. And we'll be going down to the locker room shortly, where Tommy Heinsohn will be starting the interviews. But before we do that, I have the final statistics." He went through the entire final box score, stretching it to about two minutes he wanted to kill as much time as possible.

He obviously received a signal to keep going. "It certainly was a great game tonight," he continued. "An outstanding ball game with the Celtics proving once more what an outstanding team they are. We'll be going to the locker room shortly, where Tommy Heinsohn will start the interviews with the ballplayers."

Another signal to keep rolling. "Okay," he said. "The stats for tonight are." He proceeded to run over practically the same figures he had already given. "What's that?" he asked. We've got the . . . er . . . er . . . What movie following the game?"

By then Red was ready to parachute from high in the stands where they sit the announcers and press in the Forum. "Yup," he said, "as Tommy told you, Havlicek played a great game. Which reminds me, we'll be going to the locker room shortly to join Tommy and the players."

Every thirty seconds he was hoping and praying they would be going to the locker room. "I can't imagine what's happening down there," he said. "Oh, they're not in the locker room yet. Well, the stats for tonight are . . ."

I want to tell you that Red Auerbach never spent more time in hell than during those fifteen minutes. The people at home must have thought they were listening to a broken record. They were accustomed to Auerbachisms from the booth but nothing like the night in Los Angeles when Russell slammed the door on Red's tongue.

Red had retired from coaching but not in the television booth. He would jump up and yell down to the floor, and into the microphone: "Siegfried! What are you doing that for? Now, Siggy knows he's got to go to the basket."

It made no difference that everything went over the air. "Stop coaching," I'd say. "Sit down and eat your peanuts, Red. Leave the guy alone. Besides, he can't hear you from up here, anyway."

I was the play-by-play man, but with Red, I had to be a moderator. "Red, they're really fast-breaking, aren't they?" I would cue him. "They're not running at all," he'd scream. "Why is that man calling a foul on Sam Jones? It was the other way."

I had to ask him to eat his peanuts, drink a Coke, or read a commercial to keep him from jumping to the floor, or losing his sanity. It was forty-eight minutes of fun and conflict working with him. Even the interviews weren't sacred.

One night in Philadelphia we had as our guest Frank DeFord, an excellent writer who apparently had irritated Red with one line in a long *Sports Illustrated* article. "I understand you're from Princeton?" was Red's opening. "Yes, I'm from Princeton," responded DeFord.

Poor Frank never had a chance to utter another word. By the time Red finished telling Frank why he hadn't agreed with his whole story, the second half was ready to start, and all the audience had learned about DeFord was that he had attended Princeton.

Another time Red conducted an interview in Los Angeles during the playoffs. Out there, the visiting announcers stage their interviews alongside the press area and on the landing of a stairway used by the fans to reach refreshment stands and other places. The people bump into you during the interviews—a lovely arrangement.

Red's guests were Pancho Segura and Ray Daniels and his wife, Julia Adams. Red had played tennis with Pancho that afternoon and was very friendly with Ray Danton. There was no way I could get involved with that group, so I made arrangements to cue Red for commercials.

"I'm going to be near you off camera," I told him. "When it's time to break for a commercial, I'll pull your coat." He understood and the interview proceeded. I received the director's signal for a commercial and tugged Red's coat.

Nothing. I jerked his coat a little harder. "Pancho," said Red, continuing to talk, "wasn't that a great forehand . . . ?" I yanked harder and still no reaction. I finally assumed Red must have thought he was being jostled by the people walking up and down the stairs.

"We've got to get a spot in there—we've got to get a spot," said the director, frantically. I had to do something, so I stepped on camera. "Red," I said, taking the mike, "I didn't know you were such a great actor until you came to Hollywood. You know there are people who might want to hear about all the things that make it possible for us to be here. So why don't you give them a chance to talk?"

It reached the point where the basketball game was secondary, and it became the Tommy and Arnold Show. One night the Celtics were involved with the Lakers in some accelerated action. Fast-break baskets, one after another.

At the risk of being accused of showing off, this is how I handled it: "Havlicek for two. West comes right back. Now Russell. Here comes Baylor. He counters." As I was drawing a breath, Red said: "He counters?" So I said: "What would you have wanted me to say? He tabletops?"

I guess that's why Red eventually offered me the coaching job—to get me off the air. I don't know whether it was his idea or someone simply had advised Channel 56 to do something about Heinsohn and Auerbach before it lost its license. Anyway, it was during the time of our television escapades that my relationships with Red and the Celtics were renewed and strengthened.

I was even projected into a problem Russell was having with Siegfried, an independent thinker to himself but an odd one to others. Siggy had come to the Celtics in the 1963–64 season, the season before I retired, so I got to know him very well. In fact, there was a time when Red wanted to get rid of him at the cutdown date in his second year, but I saved his job.

"If you're thinking of letting Siegfried go," I told Red, "it'd be a big mistake. Go up to the top of the stands and don't let the kid see you watching us. I've played one-on-one with this kid every day after practice, and he is the only one on the team who can beat me consistently."

Mr. Contrary, of course, had to say: "You can beat Russell?" I assured Red I could beat Russell, Cousy, Sharman, Ramsey, or any Celtic he had ever signed, but not Siegfried. So Red went high into the stands, watched the one-on-one, and admitted I was right, finally.

The problem was Siggy's attitude. He was stubborn to the point where, if he was told to do something, he would accentuate the positive to emphasize the negative. Russell couldn't handle him, and Red, believe it or not, threw up his hands and said: "I can't talk to that kid." I always knew there was something about Siggy I liked.

Siegfried had definite ideas as to what should be done and what he could do and that's all there was to it. "Look," Russell would tell him, "you're a great basketball player but when you're coming down with the ball, you've got to take some shots. You're looking to pass all the time and we've got to get some points out of you. Take the shot if you've got it, otherwise hit the open man."

Simple? Understandable? Not to Siggy. He would go out the next game and fire thirty-five shots and never pass. "Siggy," Russell would then say, "I didn't mean for you to take thirty-five shots. Take it when it's there but give it up when it's not." So the next game Siggy would go to the other extreme by passing the ball and not shooting. From Barry Goldwater to Bella Abzug—just like that.

It reached the point where Siegfried was going to solve the problem for everyone by quitting. He was going to join the ministry. He was going to get next to God. He had to get away from the emotional turmoil he was experiencing with the Celtics.

I was the only one to whom he would talk because I had been the only one to spend any time with him when I was playing. I had become his confidant. I would counsel him on how to negotiate with Red. "I'm holding out," was the discreet way he would put it to Mr. Auerbach. I advised Siggy he would hold out right back to Ohio State with that diplomacy.

Red knew we had that relationship and asked me to see if I could reach Siegfried. I was doing the telecasts at the time but it was part of Celtic family business. I was asked to get Siggy to understand that the sun set in the west, not the east, and that the Celtics understood him even if he didn't understand himself. Straighten him out was the assignment.

On the plane returning from a game, I sat next to Siegfried and unloaded on him. "Why are you carrying on about quitting?" I asked. "These people think highly of you. They think you can be a big help to the team." He thought of something. "I can't play coming off the bench," he said.

Fine, except when Siggy was a starter, he still was not overjoyed. "What do they expect me to do," he complained, "play forty-eight minutes? I need a little rest." I flattered him and itemized his playing assets. "They're expecting too much of me," he said.

I never completely resolved Siggy's problem, not then nor when I became the coach, but I was involved with team functions while telecasting and that became important. I would listen to the grumbling about the coaching, just as players have grumbled about Red Holzman, Auerbach, and even Heinsohn's coaching.

I laughed when they griped about Russell's coaching, though. That was like saying you didn't like Marilyn Monroe movies because she couldn't dance. "Are you guys crazy?" I'd tell the moaners. "You've got the greatest damn center in the league. Don't worry about his coaching—just play. As long as he's playing, you're gonna win. Stop all the griping if he has a cup of coffee at practice. Play. Don't worry about it."

I did everything but set up a confessional booth, which Auerbach would have permitted if he could have charged admission. It put me in an ideal position to be studied by Red during the Russell coaching years, which lasted through two more championships and ended after the 1968–69 season.

I wasn't there in Los Angeles when the Celtics beat the Lakers in the seventh game of that final playoff for Russell because it was nationally televised. But right then I suspected Russ was going to quit. He was thirty-five and very definitely had played in spots, saving himself for last quarters and the playoffs.

Boston had finished fourth in the East but beat the 76ers and the Knicks to gain the final. Russell appreciated his personal struggle more than anyone and was too proud to push Russell the player beyond his endurance and the horizon. He had saved himself for a last hurrah, which was obvious to me if no one else.

Then he criticized Wilt soon after the Celtics had won the series and their eleventh title in Russell's thirteen years. That's the game where Chamberlain removed himself when hurt and Butch van Breda Kolff refused to put him back after the Lakers had come from far behind to make it a game with Mel Counts at center. Russell spoke out West someplace and suggested he would have acted the same as Butch under the conditions and proceeded to ridicule Wilt's appraisal of himself.

I knew Russell was through playing and coaching because he never would have antagonized Wilt under any other circumstances. His whole approach to Chamberlain was to treat him like a pussycat. "Wilt, come over to the house for dinner," and things like that. It was interesting to watch it develop and Russell work at it. I am sure Russ never forgot the first game Wilt the rookie played against him in Madison Square Garden in 1959.

I have never seen a player play like Wilt played that night—and that includes Russell. I mean Wilt stuffed Russell, Heinsohn, Auerbach, Cousy, and everybody in his pocket and the basket. They should have written only his name in the box score because he did everything.

On a super scale Wilt was super-duper in that game. He scored, grabbed rebounds, blocked shots, and was just awesome. He was new to NBA basketball but they had whipped up a huge rivalry for him with Russell before Wilt had played an exhibition game. He had something on his mind, obviously.

Wilt was motivated by a desire to show New York what Chamberlain could do against Russell, considered the dominant figure because the Celtics had won two titles in three seasons with him. Wilt smashed everyone out of the way and controlled the game more than the referees.

It may sound absurd, but I saw the real Wilt Chamberlain play only once—that night in New York. I think that right then Russell made up his mind, or had it made up for him, that the best way to handle Wilt was with kindness. Never bring out the animal in him.

In all the years I played with Russell, and after I quit, I never knew him to say an unkind word about Wilt. I could guess what he was thinking, but Russ was smart enough to keep his thoughts to himself. Once he had words with Wilt when he threatened to attack Red but at no time did Russ ever ridicule him or join the crowd that insisted Chamberlain was a loser because his teams didn't win as often as the Celtics.

When Russell asked for a dollar more than the hundred thousand dollars Wilt was getting, it was carefully considered as no detraction. Our whole team concept was based on stopping Chamberlain, and Russell would play him tough but make sure never to arouse him. Russ avoided providing any ammunition for the writers who antagonized Wilt with their own taunting reminders of his failures against the Celtics.

Russell's pet tactic was to work like a superhuman against Wilt for three quarters of a game, hoping to neutralize or minimize him. If and when the Celtics had a game locked up, Russ would ease off and let him get his points. There was no way Russell could do that all the time because Wilt was too talented, but it was done when the opportunity was there. He was Boston Slim, the Celtic Hustler.

Chamberlain would always complain that Russell won because he had better ballplayers around him. What Wilt never recognized was that Russ made him look to his own players for support and, therefore, he became more conscious of them. That was part of the psyching. Wilt would get his forty points, with a little help from Russell, and look so good in the box score that the other players would appear bad by comparison.

That was the subtle game Russell played with Wilt. He did it for years—making sure never to deliberately anger or embarrass Chamberlain. Russell never said one word that would make Wilt mad at him and repeat that 1959 performance in New York.

Whenever we tried to discuss Wilt with him, Russell would just laugh. He didn't even trust us. He had the most to lose if anything leaked to Wilt. The only time I ever heard him talk about Chamberlain was in the playoffs, and then it was how he was going to play him.

Normally Russell would play Wilt tightly and then Wilt would lay his arm on Russell's shoulder while rolling the ball into the basket. "I'm going to bump him out," Russ said during one playoff. "Then I'm going to back off, and when he rolls to the hoop, I'm going to try to block the shot instead of letting him jam me into the ground with his arm."

Russell, with five fouls on him in a key game, blocked two shots on Wilt that way. That's the only time Russ even discussed how he was going to handle Wilt in a game. So I knew the Boston coaching job was open when Russell, in effect, blasted Chamberlain like someone who had kept his feelings suppressed for too many years.

On that basis, I engaged Red in a conversation as to Russell's future. "Red, is Russell going to be here next year?" I asked early in the summer of 1969. "I dunno," he said. "If Russell does quit," I said, "who's going to coach the club?" Red indicated he had someone in mind who could coach and also handle some of the business aspects to relieve him of some pressure.

"If you're interested, I would be interested," I advised him. "It would be fun for me to help rebuild the club after Russell is gone." Sam Jones had announced his retirement before the playoffs and I knew what it would mean to a Celtic coach starting without him and Russell.

There had been speculation about Russell returning and also going to Hollywood to play tall man romantic leads. He had the Boston press speculating wildly when, in reality, he had negotiated with *Sports Illustrated* to sell his retirement story. Red confided in me that Russ had told him he was quitting but he wasn't prepared to believe it. "I think he'll be back," was Auerbach's feeling but not mine, of course.

I read Russell's intentions better than anyone. My trained eye indicated Russ had no desire to play again, and I knew he would never operate strictly as a coach. He was a player, not a coach. He wouldn't remain only as a coach because there wouldn't be enough money in it for him.

Cousy already had been named coach of the Cincinnati Royals, eliminating him as a formidable competitor. I reminded Red of that as we discussed the situation. "You asked me once," I told him, "and now I'd be interested."

There was a five-second pause. "You've got the job," said Red. "If Russell doesn't come back, you've got it." Russell didn't come back, and I had the job.

13

WHAT? ARE YOU KIDDING? Damn. My face was contorted in anger for a change. I looked for something to kick. The towel in front of the bench. Perfect. I booted it. Oops. My shoe.

The damn loafer sailed forty rows into the stands. What an embarrassing thing to happen in front of ten thousand people in the Boston Garden, many of whom hadn't accepted Tommy Heinsohn as a coach. I had been the Celtic clown, the whipping boy, the pet target of Auerbach, Cousy, and Russell for allegedly being fat, lazy, indifferent, shot happy, and other demeaning influences on one's image.

"I wonder," I said, looking sheepish, "if anyone saw my shoe fly?" Oh, well, it was gone. Next problem: How the hell do I get it back? I did not want to be any more conspicuous than I had been, but it is difficult to hide when you are as big as I am, standing in front of the bench in full view with one shoe off, one shoe on.

I called over the ballboy. "Frankie," I said, "I kicked my shoe up into the stands and I want you to go find it." I had to convince him I wasn't joking, of course. The game was going on, which I hoped provided enough of a distraction so that not too many had noticed my predicament.

With my luck, naturally, the towel went flying with the shoe, creating a jet stream effect. It was difficult under the circumstances not to see the unidentified flying object, which did not enhance my image among those who had little faith in my ability to capably follow Auerbach and Russell, the coaches of champions.

Strange things always seemed to happen to me. In a 1974 playoff game with the Knicks, the referees were wrong, as usual, and I was off the bench twisting my face in anger, as usual. It was normal procedure, after much experience, for me to jump off the bench and walk away from the heat of the action. That would give me time to fight my temper and not the officials.

If I lost the battle, I'd scream at the refs. If I won, I'd continue to the water cooler at the end of the bench, fill a cup, take a sip, and show my dismay by dropping the water into a bucket. The ballboys had learned to hold the bucket away from them because they had been splattered often enough.

This time I was so distraught, I couldn't control my anger by the time I reached the cooler, which was plastic, fortunately. I kicked it and the contents poured onto the court. It was on national television and everyone in the country saw what I had done but not the officials —which I did not discover until later.

"Uh-oh," I said to myself. "That wasn't the smartest thing to do." I didn't want a technical in such a critical game at such a critical time. So instead of backtracking to my seat, I just kept going. I turned the corner, sneaked behind the Celtic bench and between the front row of customers, and slid into my seat at the opposite end.

By then, Mendy Rudolph had noticed the commotion near the cooler as well as the wet floor. He spotted the bucket knocked over and right away figured how it had happened. But he couldn't find me because, while he was looking toward the scene of the accident, I was out of sight—screened by the players and fans.

Again I was the big joker to the Celtic fans and press. I had to be me, but it always seemed to come out funny. Like the night I was aroused once more by something extremely serious—we were called for charging when, to me, anyway, it had been clearly blocking.

I wanted to be different this time. I had flung towels on the floor. I had kicked water coolers. I had hurled defiance. So I removed my jacket and slammed it to the floor in a vivid demonstration of disapproval of the officiating. They might not have liked my coaching but they had to admire my dramatic flair.

In the meantime, everything in my pockets went flying. My wallet, my credit cards, my bankbook, and my change scattered all over. What now? By then I had been in so many embarrassing situations, I quickly went to my hands and knees and picked it all up while the game continued. Nobody even missed me.

The players on the bench never made a move to help. They sat there and casually looked at me as though saying: "So what else is new?" They had seen it before and they knew they would see it again, in some form or manner.

One night I made an extra-special effort to stay in my seat. I had made up my mind it would take something extreme to get me excited. The newspapers had enough angry-man pictures of me in their files. It lasted about as long as it takes a referee to toss up the first ball.

I jumped up so violently, I split the back seam of my pants and we were still in the first half. John Killilea, my assistant and the Celtics' super scout, was sitting on the bench for that game, and I solicited his aid. "John," I said, "I ripped my pants up the back. Stand behind me at all times. Move when I move. Screen me out." I am sure the fans must have wondered why I sat so calmly the rest of the half.

I got right on the problem at intermission. I removed the pants and had Frank Challant, the trainer, tape the split seam together because there was no needle and thread. I wasn't about to ask Dr. Thomas F. Silva, Jr., our team physician, to stitch it up. Could you picture him taking my pants to surgery?

Challant did a fine job, qualifying him for Tailor of the Month. Meanwhile, I delivered my halftime inspirational speech to Dave Cowens, Paul Silas, John Havlicek, and the others in shirt, tie, and undershorts. Are you sure Knute Rockne or Red Auerbach started that way?

I am sure no coach started the way I did. I actually became coach of the Celtics because Russell did not show up for the job. Red had kept the door open for him to walk through until the last possible moment.

"The Celtics have a reputation for never quitting," said Red despite Russell's announced retirement as player-coach in the magazine. "Russell has never quit and I've certainly never quit. As far as I'm concerned, Bill Russell will be retired when he doesn't show up for the first day of training camp."

Some people obviously misinterpreted Auerbach's reason for saying that. They assumed it reflected a lack of faith in me as a coach when it really was Russell the player about whom Red was concerned. He realized how impossible it would be to fill Russell's spot at center and compensate for what he had done for the Celtics throughout the years, so he waited as long as he could for Bill to change his mind.

I was in a strange position when everyone gathered at Boston State College for the first day of practice in the 1969–70 season. If Russell walked through the door, he would be the player-coach. If he didn't, I was the coach. The Celtic rookies and the entire Boston media were on hand for the historic moment. They remained for my first press conference and practice session as the man who backed into the job of rebuilding the Celtics into another championship team.

I didn't mind because I was well aware of Red's thinking and sincerity. Others seemed to mind, because it took me years to convince people that Auerbach was not coaching the Celtics under an assumed name. I am not sure I have convinced all the people yet, despite one Coach of the Year recognition, one championship, and a team concept of which I am proud, anyway. At least my family thinks I coach the Celtics.

I really don't know how Johnny Most figured it out, because he was an announcer, and all sportswriters are supposed to be the experts, but the day I was named coach, he wrote an article for a Boston paper that predicted just what would happen. "To me," he wrote, in part, "Heinsohn represents the closest total of Auerbach coaching attributes of all the ballplayers who have played for him.

"I think Tommy will turn out to be a junior edition of the Redhead. He will fast break. He will torture them to superhuman rebounding efforts. He will go nose-to-nose with the officials. He will draw many technical fouls. He will be a proud advocate of wide-open, firehouse basketball, with an occasional explosion of violence. This is going to be a 'go to hell' ball club. It'll come to games ready to take the building apart in order to win."

I am thankful to Johnny Most and a few writers for recognizing what some do not recognize even today. I am not going to say that Red was not available with professional suggestions when I needed them. I am not going to say that he and I didn't go into the little office off our dressing room in the Boston Garden to review ideas as well as game developments in my first season as coach.

It was difficult for Red and me to act otherwise. We had played that type of game on the Celtics, and there was no reason to change the relationship when I became the coach and he was the president-general manager. It still was a team effort.

Red always had encouraged the players to contribute their thinking to team welfare. "I'm the only one who talks in the huddles," was his standing command. But in a sticky situation, we would huddle and Red would ask for suggestions. "Okay," he'd say, "let's use Heinsohn's play." He reserved the right to make the decision but never refused to listen.

It led to some interesting situations at times. One night we came down to the last shot. We huddled and it was suggested that we set up Sam Jones. "Okay," said Red, "it's Sam. We'll run the four play for you." Sam shook his head. "What's wrong, Sam?" Red asked. "My feet are cold," said Sam.

"Your feet are cold?" said Red, incredulously. "Forget it. We're running the play to you." Sam shook his head again. "What's wrong now?" asked Red. "My hands are cold," said Sam. We ran the play anyway, and Sam made the shot to win another game for us.

That is the way Red conducted his business with the Celtics, explaining why he was so successful. He had the public image of a dictator, yet he ran the team like a democracy, with the right to do as he pleased, when he pleased.

It was no accident that the players he trained went on to top coaching jobs in college and the pros: K. C. Jones in Washington, Bill Sharman in Los Angeles, Bob Cousy in Cincinnati, Larry Siegfried in Houston as Johnny Egan's assistant, Bill Russell the supreme boss in Seattle, Satch Sanders at Harvard, Jim Loscutoff at Boston State, Bob Brannum at Brandeis, and Frank Ramsey in Louisville with the Kentucky Colonels.

Red had a wonderful track record until he chose me as coach; then he had to explain why to the apprehensive media. He mentioned my intelligence, knowledge of the game, business mind, and dedication to the Celtics. "He has remained closely associated as a broadcaster and scout," he added. "He has the knowledge of the personnel. He is a great motivating force. We understand his problems and that he hasn't had any actual pro experience."

It wasn't sufficient. "Will you help Heinsohn?" someone had to ask Red. "Yes and no," he said. "I'll be available during practice. But once he starts the season, he's on his own. I won't be on the bench or near the bench."

Why couldn't people accept that as a sincere expression of faith in me by Red? Why was it that no one treated me with respect? Why didn't they believe in me?

I wasn't too bad-looking. I was cordial—at times. I was ready, willing, and able. I was credible. I really did see that talking dog one night in San Diego, you know.

I was out there for the 1971 All-Star game. I went as a player representative . . . no, I really don't know what the hell I was doing there. Let's just say I went because they were celebrating the Silver Anniversary team of the NBA and I had played with and against a lot of the players to be honored.

I wanted to be there, so Red paid my way. It was a wonderful vacation for me. The banquet with the celebrities, the game and the huge cocktail party after the West had beaten the East, 108–107, provided a couple of full and entertaining evenings.

Around two in the morning, I decided to go across the road to an all-night coffee shop at one of the motels in the area they call Hotel Circle. I was with Eddie Leiser, an acquaintance and dog fancier from Los Angeles, and we went to have some ham and eggs and coffee.

On the way out of the coffee shop, we ran into someone with a beautiful miniature French poodle. Eddie, of course, had to stop and admire the dog and converse with the owner. Eddie told the owner how much he loved dogs and how his dog, a Russian wolfhound, I think, always was in the car with him. "Mine's a trained dog," said the proud owner of the poodle. "He talks." He what?

I knew the hour was late and we had had a few drinks, but that was a little ridiculous. "Get out of here," was my intellectual response. "There's no such thing as a dog that talks."

"Really," the guy said. "The dog can talk." We had to find out, naturally, even if he was pulling our legs. So he sat the dog down and began talking to it. "Say I love you," he told the dog. I started to laugh but the dog went: *"Rahruvru."*

Wait a minute. "Where do you live?" the guy then asked. *"Rrrndiagrr,"* answered the dog. I couldn't believe he had said San Diego in dog language. That dog actually carried on a conversation with the guy. His diction wasn't so hot, but who expected a poodle that had gone to Oxford?

It was like that old joke: "Who hit the most homers?" and the dog would bark: *"Rrrooof!"* I really understood the dog, making me wonder a little about me. "This dog not only talks," said the owner, expanding the act, "but he has great comprehension. You can tell him to do things and he'll do it. He's like a human being."

He instructed the dog to take three turns around a nearby mailbox, pick up a piece of paper, and jump over a fire hydrant. *Voilà.* Just like that, the poodle did it.

A sportswriter friend and his wife came through the parking lot at that time and I stopped them. "You've got to see this talking dog," I said. "Oh, sure, Tommy," said the writer, looking at his watch and smiling at his wife.

The dog performed, again, and the sportswriter and his wife were impressed—I think. I was impressed, anyway. The dog was so intelligent, I'm sure he would have gone out and grabbed thirty rebounds if I had told him to do it. I'll bet that dog could've called out our plays. We only had six, you know.

It was a remarkable performance. The funniest part was the reaction of my friend, the dog fancier. After the poodle had talked, responded to instructions, and did everything but sing, my friend said: "You know, that dog has bad hind legs."

That was my problem. How could I expect anyone to believe I was qualified to coach the great Celtics when they wouldn't believe I had heard a dog talk one night in San Diego?

In my early stages as coach, I asked Red to sit at the press table alongside me in the Boston Garden for a personal reason. It had nothing to do with the players or the game. I wanted him to study my bench conduct as well as my conversations with the referees.

Red left his private box on the opposite side of the floor for four games for that specific purpose in that first season. So what happened? "Does Havlicek, Auerbach, or Heinsohn Coach the Celtics?"

was a headline that appeared in a paper as recently as the middle of the 1974–75 season. Any sign of encouraged involvement by Red or the players always seems to be interpreted as Heinsohn's coaching weakness.

I shall overcome. I readily admit that Red was invaluable at the beginning and still is in many respects. He has never lost his intense interest in the Celtics and never will as long as he is actively associated. He had quit coaching but attended practice, even when Russell was coaching, so why stop when I took over?

Red recognized I had been thrown into a difficult situation, and he offered some guidelines for practices. He would tell me I was talking too much or suggest other tactics but never interfered with the contents of the workouts. We discussed practice techniques but not coaching ideas and theories.

For example, I always had an idea about the fast break that grew out of the way Cousy ran it. I called it the six-man break because that is the way I figured it would appear to other teams. Everybody using the break figured that five on four was the maximum. My six-man concept was based on a constant flow that made it seem as though six men were involved.

At the risk of being too technical, this is the way it works: we attack a certain area of the defense by overloading it. We have two men swinging through all the time with a third rotating, which creates the illusion that there are six men attacking.

I installed it from the start, when we had Henry Finkel, Bad News Barnes, and Rich Johnson playing the middle and making everyone forget Bill Russell. We perfected it when Dave Cowens became a Celtic and added his speed and constant motion to the position. All the big men worked as the middle man on the break in every practice. That way the centers learned to handle the ball and became accustomed to the rhythm of game conditions.

I considered it innovative but few noticed such things. All that the writers ever noticed was Red babysitting at practice. They had no idea what our discussions involved. They saw us talking, so Red had to be telling me what to do.

Red's main interest was in what the players were capable of doing that season. We had lost Russell and Sam Jones, making it obvious the Celtics would not repeat their championship, though Auerbach wasn't sure about that. He wanted me to keep him advised on the manpower and, therefore, what he could do as general manager to help.

"I don't know about this team," he said to me. "We can win it or end up in last place." He missed both. We didn't win and we finished seventh at 34–48 in the Eastern Conference, which consisted of eight teams at that time. Detroit was last, thank goodness.

My first problem was to establish authority with the players. That is never too easy when you have played with some of the players—such as Havlicek, Siegfried, and Sanders. Also, my whipping boy image had been handed down from locker room to locker room.

They were aware of the time I had gone to Red years ago and pleaded for respect. "Red," I told him, "the rookies are stealing my socks and jocks. There's no respect for me because you are always ridiculing me in front of them."

Red addressed a meeting and advised those who did not treat Tommy Heinsohn with respect that they would have to account to him. Then, at the first opportunity or sooner, he chewed me out in practice or at half time during a game. That was the legendary Tommy Heinsohn to all Celtics.

That's exactly what happened when the season started and we lost my first four games as coach. We opened against Cincinnati in Boston and that was the return of the prodigal son—Bob Cousy. "Cousy was given two standing ovations before the game," wrote one writer, ignoring the ovation I, also, had received for my first game as coach.

We then lost to Baltimore, Detroit, and Atlanta, which further established my popularity and credibility as coach. Red dropped into the locker room after we were beaten by the Hawks and made a speech that leaked to the papers, further enhancing my image.

"Yeah, well, I was mad," said Red, confirming reports that he had talked to the team. "I didn't mind losing four games but what I didn't like was the way a couple of our players were performing in practice and games. They were giving us a lot of false hustle."

He then went on to analyze, by request, the team and its prospects without Russell. Why they hadn't asked me, I knew. "We don't have a top draft choice on the team," Red explained. "Jo Jo White, our No. 1 pick, is in the Marines, and won't be out until December 18, and we traded our No. 2 choice to get Emmette Bryant.

"Sam Jones has retired, and there goes twenty points a game. Tommy Heinsohn is a rookie coach, and the thing about any rookie coach is that it takes time for the veteran players to accept him. I mean, our guys know Tommy and they like him and they know he knows the game. But he still must prove his knowledge to them during a game."

I was thinking 0–82 until we finally beat Milwaukee and Kareem Abdul-Jabbar in the fifth game for my first victory. I figured I had been rather clever by using a speed team to save the game when Barnes drew his fifth personal in the middle of the third period.

Finkel also had five fouls, so I put Nelson on Jabbar and used Siegfried, Bryant, Havlicek, and Sanders with him, replacing Emmette with Bailey Howell. I knew from personal experience that Nelson had played center in college and was smart so, in that respect, he would compensate for the size he gave away.

We won on Milwaukee's court, and the next day I read how Red's timely words to the Celtics in the locker room had been partly if not totally responsible for the turnaround. Everytime Red did something in the normal pursuit of his position it was used as evidence that I had no control or authority. He was the dog, I was the wagging tail.

We went to Madison Square Garden one night and the Knicks routed us, 133–100. That was the Knicks team that destroyed the Celtics' seventeen-game winning streak with eighteen and also was to succeed us as NBA champions. Nobody on the Celtics appreciated taking a beating from the Knicks, anywhere or at any time, so when the game ended, the dressing room was closed to everyone.

I walked into the room and was politely asked if I would mind leaving because the players wanted to meet among themselves. That was not unusual with Celtic teams. It had happened to Auerbach and no one thought anything about it. When it happened to me, there was a sinister motive and interpretation.

I said a few words to the players before I departed to stand guard outside the door. "They have to get together sometimes," I explained to the press. "We used to throw Red out." Sure.

"It was nothing against Heinsohn," explained Siegfried, identifying himself as being responsible for the meeting. "He has his job but there are intangibles you can't coach, like desire, attitude, pride, dedication. They must come from within. There are a lot of guys who never played on a losing club. I'm one of them. We're champions but we're also human beings. We've got to let that be our course and guide."

Red made his appearance in the locker room after all was said and done, and that was interpreted as most meaningful. I know how I felt, but I don't think many cared at that point. It was not easy to be in charge of the decline of the Celtic empire, though I was not responsible.

I told those who cared to listen that we had three centers: Johnson, to get the tap; Barnes, to be tough; and Finkel, to fall down under the basket. I tried being funny for a change. I even said a few kind words for the Knicks, who had lived in the ghetto for so many years and were about to move to a nicer neighborhood.

"It must be sweet for the Knicks," I suggested, "after we sat on their fannies for so many years. Let them have the gloats." Red took the occasion to remind the New York people that there were times when things must be put in proper perspective. "The immensity of what the Celtics did," was his reminder, "is just being appreciated. The Knicks have a great team but they still are fighting for a one-game home edge in the playoffs. They haven't won anything yet."

He said other things to the Celtics as a reminder that they were getting paid money that could be taken away. A few nights later, Red came into the locker room after we had lost to San Francisco by eighteen points at home and took a hundred dollars from everyone but Sanders and Bryant. They escaped because Satch hurt his knee in the third quarter and left for X rays and Bryant entered the game after the damage had been done—to the Celtics, not Satch's knee.

Under the conditions, it was understandable that Larry Colaflin, the Boston columnist, interpreted it this way in his column: "Anytime a general manager—even one with Red's stature—takes charge and fines the players, he is indicating only one thing to me: that he feels tougher measures are required than the coach is using.

"Perhaps Heinsohn was going to fine the players himself. It really doesn't matter now because it was the general manager who made the move and not the rookie coach. Auerbach, of course, was well aware of the possible interpretations of his drastic penalty on the team. He knows people will wonder now if Heinsohn is being tough enough. Maybe that's why Red did it. Maybe he wants Heinsohn to get tougher."

I didn't question Red's motives then and I don't now. I made it perfectly clear to all the Celtics right away that I was the boss and they would play my way or else. If we were going to lose, we'd do it with pride. Celtics never quit and feel sorry for themselves.

It was a time when I needed a friend, and my mind wandered, for some reason, to the Moe Waxmans. I first met him when someone told me he had muscular dystrophy and was a great Celtic fan. He was confined to an iron lung and I eventually made arrangements for him to come to the Boston Garden to see some games.

He watched through a mirror attached to the iron lung and enjoyed the game as much as anyone. I would drop by the hospital in Somerville not too far from the Garden to visit once in a while. It was a tremendous thing for me.

I was fascinated by his attitude. He was a young man in his thirties with a disease he knew was fatal, yet he was vital and alive. He met this girl Mary in the hospital and she had a similar problem but they got married and shared an unbelievable outlook on life. She was in the earlier stages of muscular dystrophy and not in an iron lung at that time, but they had many precious moments together.

They weren't acting. It wasn't false courage. They accepted their destiny and faced every day with enthusiasm for life. They made every day beautiful. They helped give me a better sense of values—a more acute awareness of what was important in life.

I still have the telegram they sent after we won the 1965 title and I indicated I was retiring: "Congratulations. Good luck for future plans. Thanks, again. Mary and Moe." They had taken an active interest in me for about four years and we had developed a close relationship.

Moe Waxman died and Mary Waxman moved out of the area. I assumed she passed away because I understood her case also was terminal. Very lovely people. Real humans.

Once in a while I thought of them when I assumed I had problems. And I had problems. Picture trying to teach Finkel, new to our club, the set plays while trying to sell new coaching philosophies to Siegfried and the other veterans. The major headache was to find someone to provide floor leadership, knowing no one was capable of replacing Russell in that respect.

I looked to the backcourt and decided on Siegfried, my old friend. He was picked by default because no one else qualified. I did not want to overload Havlicek with calling the plays and concerning himself about anything but his game.

I put in a spread offense with no pivot because we had three centers who could shoot from outside. I also wanted to fast break to beat the other team up the floor. I soon found out that Siggy didn't think we could fast break. I heard him express his opinion on a plane —my appointed leader.

I was tempted to put on a uniform and show Siggy and everyone I was right, but one thing discouraged me: I couldn't run, jump, or tolerate the stress anymore. Nobody could say I didn't try, because early in the season I indulged in a full scrimmage that lasted exactly once up and down the floor.

I had to rely on my voice, the only part of me that will always be in shape. I could get loud and forceful under the proper conditions, though I consider myself a temperate and patient individual— except when I get excited.

That brings up another problem that developed with my first Celtic team. I started out with a fine relationship with Emmette Bryant, who had entered the NBA with the Knicks the same year as Willis Reed. I guess Emmette expected more playing time in the backcourt with Sam Jones gone and felt slighted when I went to Siegfried's direction.

We had an unpleasant scene in the dressing room one night and I was on the spot for the first time as a coach. Many players thought I should have fined Emmette a thousand dollars immediately. I decided to inform Auerbach. I contemplated some serious action but I wanted to sleep on it. In the meantime, the players indicated during coffee sessions I normally had with them that Bryant should be punished for insubordination.

What compounded the situation was that it happened after Baltimore had come from behind for our seventh straight defeat. The players were upset enough about that and even more so when Bryant and I engaged in our little contest. That was new to the Celtics, who only challenged people in enemy uniforms.

We had our own gripe sessions, and Bailey Howell, for example, complained about not getting the ball. But a player defying authority had never happened before on the Celtics, and it indicated a dangerous trend. There was no way I could laugh my way out of that. It demanded serious consideration and action.

I called Emmette to my room and we engaged in a man-to-man discussion. I concluded that the best approach for the moment was for him to apologize to the team before the game that night. I had made up my mind if he refused, he would be suspended the minute the players began leaving the dressing room.

Bryant apologized and I discovered later the players still thought I should have fined him. Maybe. I felt no need to take his money. I had communicated with him and he hadn't defied me. I considered it a matter of respect and he indicated he was prepared to give me that.

Naturally, I heard stories that I was too soft and Red would have fined Emmette five thousand dollars. That was part of the Auerbach legend because Red never significantly fined anyone until my first season of coaching. Once he relieved three Celtics of twenty-five dollars each for trying to be cute with him.

He caught them sneaking into the hotel on the road because he happened to be leaving early to catch a 7:00 A.M. flight to Washington, whereas the team was heading for Boston. It was around six-fifteen when he saw the three players with three female companions. "Red," said one of the players, "I'd like you to meet my cousin and two of her friends. We're on our way to church."

Red had never heard that one before but refused to give an award for originality. "Can you beat that?" he said. "If they'd kept their mouths shut, I probably would have let it go because we didn't have a game for a few days. But when they pulled that line, I fined them an extra five dollars for insulting my intelligence."

There was no way anyone could insult Red's intelligence. The officials tried it one time when the Celtics were playing the Knicks an exhibition game on Long Island and Red pulled the team off the floor. It was his team and he was going home.

Someone informed Red that was not fair to those who had paid to see two teams play an entire game. Red relented but became the first one to be fined under Walter Kennedy's new commissionership. The commissioner had just succeeded Maurice Podoloff and proceeded to hit Red with a five-hundred-dollar fine for his indiscretions.

Red accepted it calmly, naturally. I think he tried to get someone to bomb Kennedy's office or indulge in some other subtle expression of his annoyance. Red always reminded Commissioner Kennedy how he had made him by serving as the means for much attention in the newspapers on the day of his first major decision.

I was drawing attention of a different nature. We weren't winning, and the players were becoming unhappy. What does a smart coach do in a situation such as that? I made them unhappier by turning the rest of the losing season over to Jo Jo White, Don Chaney, and Steve Kuberski, the younger Celtics. It was a season to forget, anyway.

14

"THIS IS THE dumbest team I ever played on," said John Havlicek, esteemed captain of the Celtics. That unsolicited endorsement by someone endeared more in Boston than the Kennedys did a lot for my wonderful coaching image.

I needed that like President Nixon needed another autographed picture of Dan Rather. Needless to say, I could have mauled Havlicek if he remained long enough in one place to be caught. Actually, he had meant no harm and only had been expressing impatience with the way the team had been developing my second season as coach.

Havlicek does everything in a hurry, so he was in a hurry for us to once more win the championship to which he had become accustomed. I was a little more patient and a lot more concerned with the details that it takes for a young team to grow into a consistent force. I still was having a difficult time convincing people it was my team, but with or without their permission I treated it as such.

My first season had not been a total loss. I had exposed White,

Chaney, and Kuberski to the ramifications and pressures of the NBA game as well as the style of ball I intended to use. I had established an attitude for my fast break and blitz attack while losing many games.

It all started with Richie Johnson, the fastest player on the team. He was 6-9 and weighed 185 pounds and could run. Richie would come up as the trailer on the fast break, we would spread it out, and he would hit. We won some games that way and it was obvious what was missing from the offense, if we were to restore the dignity and stature that Celtic teams symbolized.

We needed a big man because we had all the other commodities. We needed someone with the speed, strength, and shooting ability to take the fast break and jam it down everyone's throat. Curiously, we got the missing part from the 1970 draft because of our poor record and a little bit of luck.

We had finished fourth from the bottom of the league while White, Chaney, and the others were picking up an education. Detroit, San Diego, and San Francisco were to select ahead of us in the draft, but the Warriors switched spots with Atlanta because of Pete Maravich.

Detroit had indicated it would make Bob Lanier the first pick in the draft, and San Diego had indicated it would not take Maravich because he was too rich for their blood and bank balance. So the Hawks dealt San Francisco the NBA rights to Zelmo Beaty, who had jumped to the ABA, for the right to name Maravich as the third pick.

Boston was to choose fourth and we had made up our minds it would be Dave Cowens. He had been scouted by Mal Graham, who had retired young as a Celtic because of a physical disability. Graham informed Auerbach that Cowens was big, fast, aggressive, and could run all night and day. In addition: "He's the best jumping white man I've ever seen." Red went to see for himself and watched Cowens play the point on defense—which meant he was pressuring the man with the ball though his nominal position was center.

Red was impressed. He wasn't sure Cowens was big enough to be a center in the NBA but was certain that he was the ideal Celtic type. Now all we had to do was get Cowens in the draft. I had only seen him on film and, truthfully, I pictured him as a big scoring forward opposite Havlicek. I wasn't the only one Cowens fooled.

We had to sweat out San Diego because we knew the players Detroit and Atlanta would be taking. I hate to think what would have happened if the Rockets had chosen Cowens instead of Rudy Tomjanovich. It is true that Rudy developed into one of the league's top forwards but I doubt if the Celtics as constituted would have won the championship with him.

Cowens, as it developed, was exactly what we needed—the missing part, the same as Dave DeBusschere had been the missing part for the Knicks. They guaranteed themselves a championship— two to be exact—when they traded Walt Bellamy and Butch Komives to get DeBusschere's poise, ball handling, shooting, defense, and quiet leadership.

We did the same when we were fortunate enough to have San Diego leave Cowens for us. Imagine what the Rockets would have been if Cowens had joined Elvin Hayes? They still might have been in San Diego, where I could visit my friend, the talking poodle—that is, if I still had the Celtic job without the benefit of Cowens' valuable services.

It is conceivable we might never have had a chance at Cowens if I hadn't decided to go with the young players or tried to make the playoffs for the playoffs' sake. Suppose I had chosen to play Bryant and Siegfried and won enough games to finish a little higher in the standings. Then what? Sometimes it's better to be lucky than good.

We ended up with Cowens because we did what we did when we did. I had prepared for him without realizing it by installing an offense without a center the year before. I knew nothing about him other than the reports I had received from Auerbach, Graham, and the way he had performed in the Rucker League and the Stokes game.

Many players from the NBA competed in the Rucker League in Harlem during the summer, and we figured it would be good experience for Cowens to play. He left a few scars on a lot of bodies. He was so fierce and explosive hitting the boards, everyone backed away from his swinging elbows. They still do. He was the MVP for the tournament as well as for the Stokes game.

The Stokes game attracted better players because it had become traditional since Jack Twyman and Milton Kutsher started it as a means of support for Maurice Stokes many years ago. Stokes, a powerful player with the Royals, had been stricken with encephalitis at the height of a career that definitely would have meant the Hall of Fame. He was hospitalized until he died of a heart attack.

Auerbach was a close friend of Milton Kutsher's and spent summers at Kutsher's Country Club in Monticello, New York, and always arranged for the Celtics to be represented at the Stokes game there. I played a few times and felt I was contributing something truly worthwhile. Besides, it was fun taking dancing lessons while all the other guys were on the golf course.

I liked dancing, painting, acting, and drinking once in a while— or more than once in a while. One night some of the fellows decided to go over to the Raleigh Hotel for a change of beers. I had no idea it was a swinging joint until I saw the bar, which looked like something out of a Knick-Celtic playoff. Mad.

I eventually managed to squeeze close to a bartender. "You're pretty big," said a damsel near me. "I'm a basketball player," I replied proudly. "What are you doing here?" she asked. "We're playing a game tomorrow night," I said. "When are you leaving?" she asked.

I took a time out to sip my beer. "Tuesday," I replied. "Why don't you stay over a few days?" she said. "Why?" I asked. "Because," she said, "my husband leaves Tuesday night." She turned to a gentleman next to her and said "Right, Harry?" and Harry said: "That's right."

I wasn't wild about Harry or his wife, so I turned away and left with the boys. Somehow the players of today do not have the fun of years ago. I don't know of anyone who engaged in the practical jokes we did. They don't even go to the movies the way we did. How boorish.

They hole up in their rooms, call room service on nineteen dollars a day meal money, and watch television. They fool around in the dressing room before a game and laugh over the Wall Street charts but, otherwise, they are more serious but not as closely knit as players of ten to fifteen years ago.

Cowens represents a perfect example of the modern basketball player. Well-paid, well-fed, a loner, and serious about everything he does. I occasionally find him walking strange streets late at night.

Once we played a game in Portland and I went out to eat with Johnny Most. We finished around two in the morning and were heading back to the hotel when we saw Cowens coming out of an alley. We strolled to the alley, looked in, and saw nothing. No door to a restaurant or club. Just plain old darkness.

Next day I asked Cowens what he was doing at two in the morning in an alley. "Just curious," was his simple answer. He was wealthy enough to drive a Mercedes-Benz but his curiosity compelled him to buy an old Chevrolet so he could rip it apart and put it together.

He had the same approach to basketball. He liked to tear players apart and put them together. Curious, you know. My first live look at him was in a three-on-three I scheduled for the summer of 1970. I worked with him and so did Sanders and so did Nelson. "We've got a horse," was Sanders' cryptic appraisal.

A horse is an animal is Dave Cowens. That much everyone could see as soon as he became a Celtic representative. He had more natural resources than these United States but they were untapped. He was raw material and, as such, intrigued Havlicek and the other veterans but also led to a certain amount of frustration.

It was not strange to see Kuberski run into Cowens or both wind up in the same area where only one should have been for the play that was developing. They were normal mistakes that stemmed from the learning process. However, Havlicek, by nature, is a perfectionist. He plays basketball by slide rule.

If a player was a fraction of an inch off his designated positioning, John would detect it and his scientific sensibility would be disturbed. That is why, for a while, he considered the young Celtic team of my second season so dumb—with malice toward none intended. I must admit they were strange—or strangers in the world of the NBA.

Where there used to be Sam Jones and Havlicek, there were White and Chaney. Where there used to be Bailey Howell and Satch Sanders, there were Finkel and Garfield Smith. That was the Celtic team that opened the 1970 exhibition season with an additional sprinkling of well-knowns such as Rex Morgan, Willie Williams, John McKinney, Hambone Williams, and Bill Dinwiddie.

"Who are these guys?" asked one of the referees at our unveiling. "These are the Celtics?" I wasn't sure myself. I started out with Smith at center and Cowens at forward. Garfield had a physique that made me think of going on a diet. He could run and jump, and I envisioned an animal at center until we opened the regular season in New York.

Cowens turned out to be the animal. Smith couldn't take the ball away from him. Cowens had made the typical rookie mistakes in the exhibition games and I expected them to continue for some time. His worst habit as a forward was the way he fanned out on a break instead of heading straight down the sidelines as the wing man.

Garfield lasted about two or three games at center, and then I moved in Cowens. We were on our way, but nobody knew it at that specific time. We now had two Havliceks perpetually running at the opposition and a team potential that even made me impatient, but I had to control myself.

It wasn't easy taking the new players by the baby formula and hand-feeding them the playing habits of everyone in the league. I had spent the entire summer studying videotapes to reacquaint myself as to the mannerisms of Lennie Wilkens, Walt Frazier, Earl Monroe, and all the others. I had no scout at the time, so I had to prepare my own scouting reports.

I was obnoxious throughout the season. I drilled the moves of every player into the heads of everyone on our team. I went over and over and over. They were accustomed to being babied in college, and I am sure they went home and told their wives about the monster coaching them.

I could see we had the talent and so could Havlicek and Nelson, our veterans, with one difference: They wanted to win before their time. I knew we weren't ready and the situation called for repetition and more repetition. I was preparing a two-year-old for a long racing career and couldn't afford to make a mistake.

Meanwhile, we were winning but weren't doing it artistically enough for some people. We weren't performing with the classic grace and effectiveness of the old Celtics, so it didn't count. We were winning with Cowens, White, Chaney, and Kuberski, practically four rookies, and people were complaining.

I put in only three plays in order to avoid complicating the complicated minds of the younger players, and that was treated with scorn. For a guy who wasn't supposed to be coaching the Celtics, I sure got it for my coaching.

"We're playing like the Celtics of old, only not with the same finesse," I announced to the world one day. What a mistake. People soon forgot about the last part of that statement and began expecting us to play like the old Celtics with or without finesse. White and Chaney were supposed to make the winning plays all the time.

One night in a game with Atlanta at home, we were leading by a point, and all Jo Jo had to do was hold the ball. But with youthful exuberance, he threw it away and the Hawks went on to score and beat us by a point. It was an aggravating defeat in every respect, and I was as annoyed as anyone.

We went to the locker room and everyone was unusually quiet. Then Red came in. "What the hell's going on out there?" he said. "These guys don't know what they're doing." I could take a hint. I interpreted that as a criticism of my coaching. I was a little upset myself, so I suggested that maybe he would like to have the job back.

It was not like Red to deliberately hurt anyone despite the mean image he projected. I know he did not realize the harm that might have been done to the authority I had worked so hard to establish. We had been so close for so long, he assumed he was helping me and the team by blowing off the way he did.

Red quickly recognized my position as well as the indiscretion of having expressed at the wrong time his great interest in the team and desire for it to perform to its capabilities. He had other things on his mind that also must have made him a bit edgy. There were problems with money involving Trans National Communications, the company that had purchased the Celtics the year before for six million dollars.

The players received their paychecks on time, but there had been some close calls, especially with the front-office help. One time the deadline was met in a most unique way. Arrangements had been made for someone in the New York office, where the company was based, to fly to Boston on a Friday and meet Howie McHugh, the Celtic publicity director, at the airport with the checks.

For some reason, probably the round-trip airfare, the company man at the New York end gave the envelope with the checks to a passenger at LaGuardia and asked him to drop it off at the airlines counter in Boston. That's what the guy did—he dropped it off at the airlines counter but told no one. He just left the paychecks and went home.

McHugh had no idea of the change in plans. He didn't even know the identity of the company man he was supposed to meet. Howie just wandered instinctively to the airlines counter and spotted the envelope addressed to the Boston Celtics. That's how the office people got paid that week. I would say that was living precariously.

We did a lot better on the floor. We ran and ran all season. My purpose was to beat the other team by attrition. Just keep the troops pouring until the other side gave in. I somehow convinced my players that the only way they were going to win consistently was by playing the game Havlicek invented: perpetual motion.

I instructed them to let me know when they were tired and I would send in a fresh player, but I wanted every minute to be wind sprints. I took Cowens aside and painted him a portrait of himself— the way I saw him, of course. "David," I told him, "you're a six-nine center. You're not a seven-footer."

I'm sure he never would have known that if I hadn't told him so (and some people questioned my mental qualifications to coach the Celtics). "David," I said, continuing my thesis, "if you're gonna play like a seven-footer, let's forget about basketball. You're gonna play center like no one's ever played it before. You're gonna make your man run up the floor so hard, he's gonna get dead tired."

I knew he liked to run, so I let him run. It's like the old Army joke of the colonel bawling out a private for not saluting and the soldier saying: "Colonel, you've got a good job so don't screw it up." I wasn't going to screw up Cowens by getting too smart.

The first time I saw him in the 1970 training camp he was a six-nine Havlicek and he hasn't stopped running yet. All I had to do was wind him up, which is how I made Cowens the new Bill Russell of the Boston Celtics.

I had only one serious problem with Cowens. He wouldn't take the outside shot. "You've got to take them," I pleaded. "But I can't hit 'em," he said. "Take 'em and miss 'em," I said, "but take 'em. The more you miss now, the more you'll make later." Before the youngsters get too excited with that philosophy, let me explain it works best for those who have talent.

My coaching efforts with Cowens and his shyness brought out the team instinct in the other players. They told Dave he had to shoot. They wanted him to understand they would not consider him a gunner like someone I had known quite well in my playing days.

We were running more than anyone could expect with such a young team, but critical stories still were appearing. We're not going fast enough. We don't have enough plays. Sure the Celtics were winning, but they didn't have a set offense.

What could I do? Tell them to complain to Coach Auerbach? We went on to win forty-four games. Not bad at all from my point of

view. We had as much right to do that as I had to hawk some of the
hundreds of paintings I have in the Boston Garden some night.

We wound up with the seventh-best record in the league in
1970–71 after having finished eighteen games under .500 the season
before. We didn't make the playoffs, though, and that became the
biggest thing to hit New England since Paul Revere beat the British
over six furlongs. Tommy Heinsohn, who was not coaching, was a
lousy coach.

There were many disappointed people in Boston, especially the
players' wives. "We've got to make the playoffs," Kathy Finkel had
said. "Hank and I will have a baby at that time and, with hospital
bills being what they are, we can use the money."

"We're on our way back," Jackie Chaney had said. "Two years
ago the Celtics won the championship and everything that goes with
it. Last year we missed out on the playoffs. I didn't like last year."

"I think we can make the playoffs," Diane Kuberski had said.
"But I would like to read more about the Celtics of now instead of
the Celtics of old."

Good girls . . . oops, woman persons, all of them. The Celtic
family attitude touched all the wives through the years. They started
a ritual when I was playing that exists today. Anytime a player with
tenure left the team, the wife was thrown a party and given a gift.

When Diane was a player's wife, they would give the departing
wife gold jewelry that was inscribed: "From the Girls on the Row."
When Chaney announced he was leaving the Celtics after the
1974–75 season, the wives threw a party for Jackie and gave her a
charm that I believe had this inscription: "The Celtics' Loss is St.
Louis' Gain."

A happy wife makes a happy player, and the Celtic wives always
have worked at being close. When I was playing, they would trade
off, helping each other whenever anyone got sick. Missy Cousy
would leave her two kids at home to help Diane with our three kids
and so on down the line of wives and kids.

I remember the night Missy Cousy came to our home because
Diane had a strep throat she probably picked up while sitting with
someone else's kid. She cooked and helped keep me isolated from
my wife. The doctor examined Diane and, almost before advising
her to remain in bed because her throat was terribly infected, he
suggested I leave the room.

"You've got to get out," implored the doctor. "You're in the playoffs." He showed more concern that I might contaminate the other Celtics than for poor Diane. The Celtics were just one big family in Boston. As long as the team was of championship quality, of course.

Auerbach and I thought of that every minute and every day and were certain it was just a matter of time. How much time depended on how fast Cowens, White, and Chaney developed. We led the East with a 56–26 record for the 1971–72 season, but the Knicks knocked us out of my first playoffs in three years as a coach, four games to one.

I should have been disappointed but I wasn't because I saw the team growing. The players were inconsolable after the Knicks won the final game in the Boston Garden. I never saw a more depressing locker room. They had expected so much of themselves and then nothing.

Red and I had evaluated the situation long before the playoffs and came to the same conclusion: We needed a power forward. The way Cowens played the game, we needed someone to protect the boards while he was chasing guards, forwards, and centers all over the place.

To know what you want is easy, but to get what you want—well, you need intelligence and patience.

That's how we got Paul Silas, the answer to our schemes. It was a combination of Red's masterful way of doing things and Jerry Colangelo of Phoenix coming forward at the right time to suggest a deal for Charlie Scott, who had been playing in the ABA.

I remember the night Colangelo came to Madison Square Garden when we were playing the Knicks during the regular season to talk with Red about Scott. I think Jerry went to Boston the next day to continue the discussions with Red on his home court, where he's more dangerous. Colangelo was the one who initiated the talks and pressed them, while Red played it cool and not too anxious.

We had surveyed the power forwards, and Silas was the player we had preferred from the Phoenix roster but we had no idea we could get him. We never realized the NBA rights to an ABA player would draw Silas from the Suns.

Red had made Scott a throwaway pick late in the 1971–72 draft. Charlie had signed with the Virginia Squires with eligibility left at North Carolina but was not eligible for the NBA draft until a year later, when his class graduated. The ABA appeared shakier to Red in those days, so he decided to stake an NBA claim to Scott on the fifth round in case the league folded. Never did a man do so much with so little.

Red never expected Charlie to rush things by discovering a loophole in his Virginia contract that led him to Phoenix. By then the deal for future delivery of Silas to the Celtics had been worked out to everyone's satisfaction—especially ours.

Silas finished the season with the Suns while Scott joined them for six games. We could afford to wait until the following season because of the transaction Red had managed. He required the Suns to sign Silas to a new contract before the Celtics' first exhibition game. He also required them to pay the difference between what the Celtics wanted to pay Silas and what the Suns eventually signed him for in a four-year contract.

There was another thing Red negotiated with the Suns. If Silas was not delivered on time, Phoenix was obligated to send the Celtics a designated substitute from its roster. That player would remain with the Celtics after Silas reported, which would have made it two players for Scott, who cost the Celtics nothing but a few chosen words by Auerbach.

Phoenix escaped the penalty by getting Silas to our training camp when it opened. Red then traded Paul Westphal to the Suns for Scott after the 1974–75 season, which meant the Celtics wound up with Silas and Scott for Westphal. How could a coach lose with a general manager like that?

It wasn't all that simple, though. We almost lost Silas before we got him. In the summer of 1972, Trans National Communications, the company that owned the Celtics, was forced into bankruptcy. As I understand it, Colangelo came close to buying Silas back from the Celtics in order to meet the demands of creditors.

Red had to do some fancy maneuvering with the league to save Silas. The Celtics were soon to be under the new ownership of Robert J. Schmertz, a lovely man who died long before his time a few months after the 1974–75 season. I'll always remember Bob as a sports enthusiast whose desire to be totally involved with the Celtics was catered to when Red let him personally make the tenth pick in the draft every year.

We were a different and better team with Silas wearing the uniform of the green in the 1972–73 season. I know I'm going to surprise a few people when I say we had more reason to win the championship that season than we finally did by beating Milwaukee in our NBA title year in 1974.

We played perfect ball soon after Silas made us stronger and deeper as a team. We had by far the best record in the NBA with 68–14—only one short of the 1971–72 Lakers' sixty-nine record wins. We won at home, on the road, the close games, the come-from-behind games, and the impossible games.

We won so much and with such finesse and finality that people lost their heads and voted me Coach of the Year. I had to inspect the award to make sure my name was on it. I was pleased because it was the first true recognition of the hard work, emotion, temper tantrums, and infrequent smiling I had invested over four strenuous years.

Yet it didn't mean much after we defeated Atlanta, four games to two, and the Knicks, the eventual champions, eliminated us, four games to three, in the Eastern Conference final. I can be totally objective where the Celtics are concerned, so let me say right now that the Knicks were not the better team that season, nor in the playoffs, for that matter.

By then the Knicks-Celtics games had become holy wars. There was devout fanaticism in both Gardens, with the decibel battle rising in direct ratio to the intensity of action on the court. The Knicks had an edge in that respect because they had won a championship in 1969–70 and most of the players from that team were still with them. Madison Square Garden was worth a lot of points to them.

I hear people discuss the advantages of home crowd noise all the time, but they do not understand the true nature of the impact. Crowd noise does not grab championship players by the throat. It never hurts a team after it has won a title. There was no better evidence than the Celtics' improvement on the road after we won the championship in 1974. The animosity of the home fans actually inspired us to beat their team even more.

It was all new to White, Chaney, Cowens, and even Silas when we lost to the Knicks in seven games. Therefore, I do not underestimate the effect the Knick fans had on the pivotal game of the series: a double overtime 117–110 defeat that gave the Knicks a lead of three games to one.

We played without Havlicek because he had hyperextended his right shoulder colliding with Dave DeBusschere in the third game at home, which we lost as Hondo worked the fourth quarter with one arm. Two days later, in the fourth game, we led, 76–60, despite the Madison Square Garden noise, and then gave up the ball seven straight times without a shot this way: four bad passes, two offensive fouls, and a three-second violation.

I said a lot of angry things about the officiating after we lost that game that I prefer to forget. I do remember saying: "I never alibi but . . ." and then I released the tremendous frustration of losing such an important game after the players had performed so superbly without Havlicek and despite the crowd hostility.

I can recall every word I used that night, but I would rather tell an Auerbach story that illustrates what happens in a coach-referee confrontation. Red was a lot funnier on that occasion than I was when we lost that aggravating game to the Knicks.

We were playing Cincinnati at home and Oscar Robertson took a shot at the buzzer to end the half. It was late—really late. It was about a second late, but Sid Borgia allowed the basket. Auerbach, looking like the middle man on our fast break, took off after Borgia at the other end of the court. The reason why I remember the incident so well was because I always had to pull Red away from an official—most of the time because I was involved and he came out to defend me.

Sid and Red really went at each other. It looked like mouth-to-mouth resuscitation with Borgia the drowning man. Red's favorite trick was to get close enough so he could spray the referee and force him to back up. In those days, they permitted the coaches to have their friendly disputes with the refs as long as there was no cursing. Now they fine you if you don't put your hand out when you're making a turn.

"The basket was late," Red kept screaming as Borgia looked around for a windshield wiper. Sid retreated before the surging Red sea and pretty soon they were out the door and into the lobby of the Garden—the area near the employees' entrance and the men's room. That's where the officials dressed in those days, and Sid was trying to escape behind a friendly door while exchanging pleasantries with Red.

I tagged along because I didn't want Red to do something foolish and it was just too interesting to leave before I found out who got the girl. "You are terrible, Borgia," Red shouted. "How could you allow that basket? It was a second late. There's no way that thing should have counted."

When Red realized he was not winning, he got into personalities. "Borgia," he yelled, "you've got an ego bigger than you are. Why can't anyone talk to you?" Sid returned the abuse in kind, but Red said something that appeared to be the *coup de grâce.*

I think Red mentioned something to Sid about having no hair. He might have called him a bald-headed something or other. Borgia avoided the obvious reply and snorted: "Auerbach, if that broad you married didn't have money, you'd be nothing."

Red pulled back and his eyes widened as his nimble mind struggled for the appropriate comeback. "What the hell are you talking about?" he finally screamed. "She didn't have a nickel when I married her." End of argument.

I chased Jake O'Donnell and Jack Madden to their dressing room on my significant night in Madison Square Garden, suggesting they should be ashamed of themselves, among other things. Basketball has a way of destroying one's equilibrium and sanity, assuming you have those qualities to start with.

I explode as easily or easier than the next person, but I try to forget once it is over. That fourth game with the Knicks is difficult to forget even now. What made it worse, and therefore more indelible, was the way we won the next two games to send the series into a seventh game, which we lost in Boston.

Havlicek forced himself to play as we won the fifth game at home and then beat the Knicks and their fans to make it 3–3. I'll say this for the people in New York: They rooted for their team with fanatical devotion, yet when Havlicek walked across the floor in street clothes prior to the fourth game, they gave him a wild, standing ovation. They weren't all bad.

Our fans in Boston are just as loud and solidly behind us, but not when we play the Knicks. In recent years, New York kids have flooded the colleges in Boston so that when the Knicks come to town, they have a large vocal representation that makes strangers wonder how come Celtic fans are rooting against their team.

This phenomenon has been matched by the pure Celtic enthusiasm generated in Boston since, not because, I became coach. In my playing days, which, of course, was the heart of the eleven championships in thirteen years, we did not sell out the Boston Garden that often. Neither did we trigger anything like the excitement that followed the Knicks' first championship in 1969–70, which produced enough books to fill the Natick public library.

I guess Russell and the other players spoiled Boston by winning too often. Cowens, White, Chaney, and even Havlicek and Nelson, who had been on championship teams, represented a fresh approach and a new challenge. They finally created a small degree of hysteria in Boston.

People camped out in the North Station concourse at 5:00 A.M. for tickets to the final game with the Knicks that went on sale five hours later. Thousands created a huge traffic jam outside the Garden for the heaviest single-game sale in the history of the Celtics. It was marvelous to know you were partly responsible.

Unfortunately, we lost the game. Red Holzman closed the trap on Havlicek by having his players challenge him when he was dribbling and sag off him on defense. We had nothing left for the final game. I went around our locker room congratulating the players for a great season when it was over. I would have preferred being home in my cellar, adding to my art collection.

I felt sorry for Cowens, White, Chaney, and Silas. They had played so hard and so well and had deserved their first championship rings. I heard Jo Jo telling someone: "We played as hard as we could. We did better than we did last year. This series could have been over without this game ever being played if a few things hadn't happened."

I wasn't the only one who felt if not for Havlicek's injury and that damn double-overtime defeat in the fourth game, we and not the Knicks would have won the championship that year.

Noble and true, but what did it all mean? Should have, would have, could have. We were the best team for eighty-two games of the regular season but did not win the championship. We had to do it all over again.

15

I HAD A cigar in my mouth and Havlicek was pouring champagne on my head. We had just won our championship by beating the Milwaukee Bucks in game seven of the 1974 playoffs, and the world had gone mad in the tiny visitors' locker room that was jammed with wall-to-wall people.

A year later, I walked across the floor at the Capital Centre to congratulate the Washington Bullets and came upon a similar scene in their more spacious locker room. They had just beaten the Celtics in the sixth game of the 1975 Eastern Conference playoffs and were celebrating as though they had just won the championship.

I suspected at that moment the Bullets were going to lose the final series to the Golden State Warriors, whose hunger for the title was to be greater than Washington's thirst. I waded through the spraying champagne and noticed Mike Riordan and Wes Unseld off in a corner, watching in disbelief and no doubt thinking the same as I: "They've won nothing yet."

Basketball games are won or lost on the floor by the players, but attitude is so important. I could tell we were going to win the seventh game and the championship from Milwaukee just as I could tell we were not going to beat Washington in the playoffs the following season. Behavior patterns are quite revealing to coaches, who in effect are the psychiatrists of the pro basketball industry.

By the start of the 1973–74 season we had blended all the personalities and attitudes on the Celtics into one energetic force. We dominated the Eastern Conference for the third straight year despite a changing scene that saw the Buffalo Braves, a young team with power that had been built by master architect Eddie Donovan, begin to assert themselves.

We finished with a 56–26 record, second only to Milwaukee's 59–23 in the Western Conference. We had a team that gained even more respect by accelerating our defense with an all-court press. Even the coach was receiving some recognition from the impact the Celitcs were having on the pro basketball world once more, as evidenced by this "Dear Tommy" letter:

"I am still following you on TV and cheering for you. It just seems so very long ago since you sat in my senior math class and did so very well in that course. Now you are doing a terrific job as coach and I am very proud of you.

"My only fame with my students is that I taught Tommy Heinsohn. That makes me a celebrity.

"Tommy, remember me to your wife and family. They, too, must be very proud of your accomplishment.

"Perhaps, if you are in Madison Square Garden next season, you would send me some tickets for my nephews, who are Benedictine and Columban priests.

"My prayers and proud heart are with you, Sister Helen James."

I had to keep reminding myself there was more to life than just basketball games. I was dealing with people, not machines. I was responsible for directing the attitudes and talents of twelve Celtics to the job of finishing first in the eighty-two-game regular season, then having them maintain their concentration and desire through the second season they call the playoffs.

I had no trouble with incentives through the 1973–74 season because the Knicks had eliminated us in the previous playoffs so painfully and we had not won a championship yet. There was the customary heckling of Heinsohn for not using his bench and other insignificant things, but I had become immune or accustomed to criticisms by then.

When you deal with people as long as I have, you learn about people. I remember how the old Celtics would ridicule me about my painting in my rookie season. I read books, went to museums on the road, and finally decided to attend my first formal art class.

That did it. They really kidded me until I advised them as to what had happened that day. How a young lady had walked in and stripped in the middle of the room. When they heard of the nude artist's model, I had many offers of company for my next class. I could have sold tickets.

The Celtics of 1973–74 had no nude models to inspire us—only scantily dressed huge basketball opponents with an equal desire to prevail over forty-eight minutes of scheduled combat every game. I tore off my jacket, kicked loose objects, threw towels, and otherwise comported myself as an unsmiling but involved coach as we compiled another winning season. My wife suggested that my kids came to the games because they enjoyed watching me on the bench. Everytime the referee called a foul on the Celtics, they would look at me for the show and some laughs. I told Diane that was a fine way for her to bring up our children.

I wanted them to know their father as the smiling individual they saw around the house, not the distorted version that performed on the Celtic bench. Anyway, what was so bad about it? We made the playoffs again, and had the good fortune and ability to dispose of Buffalo first and then the Knicks, in that order but not in the order of ease.

Bob McAdoo of the Braves pushed us six games before Jo Jo hit two free throws with no time left to win that series for us, four games to two. McAdoo reminded me of a kid named Tommy Heinsohn the way he pumped shots from the distant reaches of the floor. Sometimes, it seemed, he hit from outside the arena, surpassing my NBA distance record from the locker rooms.

I don't know of anyone his size in the history of basketball who has had the uncanny shooting ability of McAdoo. He is basically a forward but the Braves have used him at center because they could find no one better. He scored forty-four points to tie the series at two games apiece, and forty points in the losing final game.

New York was not that difficult and, in a sense, it was disheartening to see the rise and fall of a team that had done so much to merchandise pro basketball. Dave DeBusschere and Jerry Lucas had announced they were retiring, and Willis Reed was being used only a few minutes a game because of a bad knee that would force him to quit before his time.

DeBusschere tore a stomach muscle in the second game of the series and was of no use to the Knicks after that. "We can't have any sympathy for them," said Nelson, considering DeBusschere and Reed, mainly. "Did they have any sympathy for us last year when Havlicek got hurt?"

Sympathy is to be saved for the proper time, such as when Cowens went into the Knick locker room to shake hands with DeBusschere after we had won the series, four games to one. There was too much at stake for premature compassion. Havlicek and Nelson were getting older and wanted another championship. Cowens, White, Chaney, Silas, and the others were seeking their first.

That is why I offered no artifical stimulation to drive the Celtics. I studied the films and provided the game plan and just let their natural desire take its course. If anyone was going to beat us, it would have to be a superhuman effort over forty-eight full minutes or more. The Celtics were primed for their first championship since Russell had retired and taken Sam Jones with him.

We made it against Milwaukee but almost didn't because of Kareem Abdul-Jabbar. "The team that wins this series will have its hands full with the Milwaukee Bucks," I cautiously projected before playing the Knicks. "The team that wins this series," said Auerbach recklessly, "will be the new NBA champion." Always one step ahead of me.

I was attracting attention as the coach of the Celtics. A stewardess actually took time away from the players to talk to me. "Has anyone ever told you that you look like Ernest Borgnine?" she asked. People began noticing the split between my teeth, the pug nose, and telling me I looked like Borgnine. I guess it came from all the exposure television gave me while I was playing Borgnine in "The Troubles of Tommy Heinsohn, Coach," on the bench.

My acting became more serious and dramatic as the series went through games one, two, three, four, and five. I was at the films everyday, trying to pick out a piece of strategy with which to confuse the

Bucks. I am sure Larry Costello searched for ideas to confuse us as well.

We made changes here and there, but our fundamental plan was to try to panic the Bucks with a full-court press. It was a wonderful opportunity for Costello and me to prove that basketball teams needed coaches more than, for example, baseball teams need managers.

We did such outstanding jobs, Milwaukee won twice on our court and we won three times out there, including the final game. Now, that took superior coaching in a sport that was supposed to be fundamentally home court. I must say, however, that Costello surprised me a little when he won the sixth game in Boston Garden.

Milwaukee adjusted to our press by giving the ball to Oscar Robertson to bring up by himself while the others cleared down the floor. From that point on it was execution. They executed and they won. We executed and we won.

We won the fifth game in Milwaukee and went home with a 3–2 lead and a chance to end it. We had settled down to a definite pattern, and I had no intention of making any radical changes. We wanted the Bucks working every minute to keep the stress on them, so we weren't going all the way with our fast break every time. It was no time to gamble by going to the hoop with everything.

Costello's strategy was more obvious. When stuck, give it to Abdul-Jabbar. "We're going to win it," I predicted on the plane home for the sixth game. "Even if they play well and win the sixth game, we're still gonna win it. If we can't go back to Milwaukee and win it, then we don't deserve to be champs."

We played well and won the sixth game until there were three seconds left in the second overtime. Havlicek had put us in front with a long jumper, and just like that we were the losers in the only way the Bucks could have beaten us. We pressured the ball and broke up the play Costello had designed for Jon McGlocklin during a time-out.

When stuck, give it to Abdul-Jabbar. They gave it to him off the broken play and he wheeled to the end line for a sky hook that went cleanly through as the buzzer sounded. I stood there in the Boston Garden with my mouth open and my hands pressed to my head in anticipation of a huge headache. Unbelievable, that's what it was.

There was dead silence as though the Boston fans felt more than a game had just been lost. Abdul-Jabbar had thrown the switch on them. "Sorry, Tommy," some said as I headed for the locker room. Sorry because we might lose the seventh game now that we had to go back to Milwaukee? Never.

I felt that way and I knew the players felt that way as I looked around the room. We were a championship team, and now was our opportunity to prove it. "I'm a little disappointed that we lost," I said, "but so what? We are going out to win it."

That was the critical moment for me. I had to be mostly concerned about how the players would react to adversity. The old Celtic teams always responded with Havlicek stealing the ball or Sam Jones bouncing the winning basket off the rim and through like a Yo-Yo or Russell blocking a shot.

They never went into an important game without a positive attitude, and I searched for similar signs among the new Celtics. "We feel we can beat them out there," said Cowens, without quivering or doubt. "It's always disappointing to lose," said Havlicek, our leader, "but we're not out of it by any means."

I was convinced they meant it, which is why I assured John Killilea on the plane to be ready to get drunk in Milwaukee. I knew we were going to win it after we held our team meeting to discuss the game plan for the final battle for championship rings.

I never saw such enthusiasm and desire to be involved in preparations. The players had all kinds of suggestions. That was the type of involvement I had encouraged at every opportunity. I always asked players for their ideas but reserved the right to make the final decision.

That's the way a coach should operate. I know there are many coaches who are a law unto themselves. I also know that Auerbach and Red Holzman never discouraged an input from a player, and I consider them the two outstanding coaches I have known in the pro game. I was never too bashful or proud to listen to the players and then say: "Okay, let's use Havlicek's play" or "Let's use Nelson's play." I considered that a strength, not a weakness.

I was my own coach, but democracy has a tendency to deceive people. It was interpreted as a lack of confidence and knowledge when, in truth, it was my recognition that twelve brains are better than one in a team effort. I was willing to listen to anyone as long as the idea made sense and I thought it would help the Celtics win.

There is a calculated risk you take when you accept advice from players, but that is related to the size of your ego. My ego was big but not huge enough to obscure my vision so that I couldn't detect or would refuse a good suggestion when offered. That's exactly what took place with the strategy we devised to stop Abdul-Jabbar in the championship game.

Cousy, Killilea, and I went with our wives to Auerbach's office after Kareem had shocked the Celtics in the sixth game. Cousy, Carl Braun, and Richie Guerin had been playing golf in Florida, watching our playoff games with Milwaukee on television and wondering why we weren't fronting Kareem.

"We couldn't understand it," Cousy said to me. "We're saying: Put Cowens in front of Jabbar to keep him from getting the ball." I informed Cousy that Cowens had fronted Kareem and gotten into foul trouble because of it. The strategy was not new and it would be disastrous if Cowens fouled out because we would have no games to make it up.

Then it hit me. Strategy is a matter of timing, and maybe it was the proper time to front Kareem purely as an element of surprise. "You know, John," I said to Killilea, "that could be a helluva idea for this game. Suppose we surprise them by putting Cowens in front of Jabbar and putting Silas down low behind him to cover?"

Killilea, thinking like a scout, wondered what would happen to Cornell Warner if Silas dropped off him. "Who'll cover him?" he asked. "No one," I said. "In the seventh game of the championship, on national television and in Milwaukee, instead of letting Jabbar shoot the ball, we're going to give Cornell Warner the opportunity to achieve greatness." So while Cowens and Silas pressured Kareem, we had the pleasure of seeing Warner score one point in twenty-nine minutes. The strategy was perfect because they had no time to adjust to the surprise defense.

The next day I saw pictures of Havlicek emptying the contents of a huge champagne bottle on my head as well as other wild scenes from the winners' padded cell. I also saw this headline: "Cousy Strategy Saves Celtics." I didn't give a damn but I had to smile, believe it or not, because they now had Cousy coaching the team.

I had been on many championships as a player, but there was nothing like my first as coach. I didn't mind having each player walk

over and spill a little champagne on my head. In fact, I was so emotionally exhausted it saved the trouble of lifting a heavy bottle and
enabled me to sip the bubbly wine as it rolled down my face and into
my mouth.

Underneath that liquid cascade was the smile of the real Tommy
Heinsohn. I was happy for me, my family, Auerbach, Bob Schmertz,
and every player who had contributed to the rebirth of the Boston
Celtics. I was happy for Cowens, Chaney, White, Silas, Finkel,
Westphal, and the others who had never experienced the exhilarating
feeling of winning a championship—the ultimate high in the wonderful world of sports.

Mrs. Silas put it in the proper perspective for those involved in
their first championship. "I remember that awful feeling last year
when we lost in the seventh game to the Knicks," said Carolyn Silas.
"It was a year when Paul and I thought we were going to be with a
championship team for the first time. We had always been friendly
with athletes who played on championship teams.

"We were in St. Louis and knew Bob Gibson when the Cardinals
won the World Series and were friendly with Reggie Jackson in
Phoenix when Oakland was a winner. It seems as though we were always in the stands watching someone else win titles until today."

We were greeted by some four thousand people at Logan International Airport when we arrived in Boston as the champion Celtics.
The next day there were around thirty thousand on the streets for the
customary motorcade that had been missing for so long. The Celtics
were No. 1 in the hearts of Boston and in the pro basketball world
again—but not for long.

We won the Eastern Conference crown for the fourth straight
time in the 1974–75 season but had to wait until Houston eliminated
the Knicks to play. We had drawn a bye under the change in the
playoffs, which enabled the Knicks to qualify as the wild-card team,
along with us, Houston, Washington, and Buffalo.

I concluded we were at the disadvantage because of the long
layoff as well as playing the Rockets, an easier opponent, while
Washington sharpened itself by struggling for its soul against Buffalo.
I was convinced we had a fine chance of losing to the Bullets after
our strategy meetings were treated with almost total indifference by
the players.

There were no signs of the enthusiasm of the year before, when the players strained for ideas that would help beat the Bucks in the final game. Nelson and White had gone to the blackboard and diagramed new last-second plays because Milwaukee was familiar with our others. This time the players listened but offered no suggestions. It was as though they were totally prepared in every respect to dispose of Elvin Hayes, Phil Chenier, Mike Riordan, Kevin Porter, and Wes Unseld.

We were taken out in six games and I was further convinced how hard it would be for any team to win two NBA championships in a row these days. Times had changed since the Celtics of the Russell era, mainly because expansion had made it difficult for one team to dominate the league anymore.

I think it would be impossible for any present or future team to approach the Celtics' record of winning eleven championships in thirteen years under any conditions. I'm sure they said the same thing about the Yankees until the Oakland A's came along to string together a few titles. I do believe the old Celtics could step into the league right now and repeat what they did for so many years assuming Russell, Cousy, Sharman, Heinsohn, Sam Jones, Frank Ramsey, and K. C. Jones could make a deal with Mother Time— the freedom movement, you know.

Yes, the Celtics were a legend in their time. A team that established pride, discipline, and a spirit that reached out to all parts of the country with magnetic appeal—that is, until a young man named Bennie Clyde became the first player of knowledge to ever refuse to play for the Celtics.

Until I became aquainted with Bennie, I was able to handle the different personalities the Celtics attracted through the rebuilding years. Bad News Barnes, a likable guy, would always complain that I'd let him play until the last three minutes but wouldn't allow him to finish a game. I convinced him he was earning his money by doing what I asked of him, though he eventually talked himself off the team by determining his value at sixty thousand dollars and insisting on it.

Bennie was our fifth-round draft choice in 1974 but had a most impressive training camp so we decided to keep him on the roster. He had been born in Albany, Georgia, and attended high school in St. Petersburg, Florida, where he was All-State and All-America, and then All-America for two years in junior college.

He appeared to be the perfect Celtic type. He was fast, intense, a good shooter, and had fine size at six-seven. He had been a malcontent at Florida State and eventually left college by request because he would not attend classes. His only friend was a basketball. That's the only thing he trusted.

We knew about his background because of an article in *Sports Illustrated*. He was pictured as an exceptional athlete who just couldn't avoid trouble because of character defects. I did some investigative work and found out he was a product of a complicated home and had been brought up under the guidance of a teacher.

Red and I discussed Bennie thoroughly and decided he deserved a chance on the basis of what he could do in pro basketball and what it could do for him. I spent more time talking with Bennie than with any other player on the team. I considered him an exceptional talent and a rehabilitation project at the same time. I felt compelled to help him as a player and person.

I couldn't, of course, play him too often because he was a rookie and he had so much to learn about the Celtic method of playing basketball. That's where the trouble started. One night in Hartford—I think we were playing Houston in a regular-season game—he played about eight minutes and I took him out. He never got back in and I went to him after the game to explain why. I was always explaining why because I was trying to establish some faith and trust with him.

He greeted my attempt to be objective and candid with one word. "Bullshit!" he said, loud enough for everyone in the room to hear. I backed off because I felt he was too new at the game and too confused for me to make it an issue at that point.

I let it go as though nothing had happened, knowing that the other players were well aware of the situation and would not consider it a sign of weakness on my part. I continued to use Bennie as I saw fit whether he understood it or not, though I did resume trying to patiently explain things to him.

Then one night in Madison Square Garden, we had a big lead on the Knicks with four minutes to go and I told Bennie to go in. He refused. Basketball was his whole life, but he figured four minutes when a game was over would be too embarrassing.

I didn't say a thing after the game but informed Auerbach that I no longer wanted Bennie on the team. Bennie had only one chance to survive—if he came to me and showed some sign of remorse. He had pinned me against the wall for a second time in front of the players, and there was no way I could let him get away with that— no matter how much sympathy I had for the terrible influences of his background.

I gave Bennie the next day and the next night, when we played in Philadelphia. Not a word from him. I made up my mind that he was going to be dropped from the roster to make room for Phil Hankinson, who had undergone knee surgery but was ready to contribute something in the playoffs if needed. There was only one problem: I couldn't forget a little scene involving Bennie in our locker room one day.

Silas, White, and Nelson were discussing some things that happen in military service. They were exchanging stories about policing the area, doing KP and other examples of menial military life. Bennie stepped up and volunteered that no one could make him do such things.

He was informed that his attitude would land him in the stockade. They were all joking. But not Bennie. "The guy who did that to me," he said sternly, "would have to sleep sometime, wouldn't he?" That would be the time he would get even. In other words, don't cross him if you wanted to sleep peacefully.

I recalled Bennie's ominous attitude when it came time for me to let him know I was dropping him. I asked Auerbach if he could be with me when I informed him because I didn't want to be alone with Bennie. I had fought Wilt, Meschery, Naulls, and other NBA giants, but there was something about Bennie that frightened me.

Red told me he had to go home to Washington so he wouldn't be accompanying us to Boston. I had to tell Bennie by myself. How? Where? I avoided it on the plane because that left little room to escape should there be violence.

I waited until we landed at Logan International Airport and, as we walked into the terminal, I asked Bennie to join me in the coffee shop where it was wide open and there were lots of people. Besides, I had spotted a state trooper with a nice holster, in which there was a nice gun. That's how I managed the courage to tell Bennie. He no longer was an active Celtic.

He took it calmly, thankfully. That surprised me and led to a slightly altered regard for him. Red and I decided to give him another chance. We invited Bennie to attend practices and even come to the break-up dinner after we had lost to Washington in the playoffs. We wanted him to feel as though he still was a Celtic, hoping it might influence him to be more receptive and co-operative.

It was not racial with him by any means. Bennie did not trust black or white. He wouldn't let anyone on the team get close to him. He was a loner in every respect. We assumed we could show him we were sincere and loyal by offering an opportunity to remain involved with the Celtics despite what had happened.

He never showed up at the break-up dinner and explained that a friend came to town so he couldn't attend. Red was furious at that display of disloyalty and lack of consideration for his teammates and swore he wanted no more of Bennie. I appealed to Red's better instincts and, five days after the dinner, he had Bennie in his office to discuss a new opportunity. Just one more time.

Red talked to Bennie for forty-five minutes and offered a raise that was more than I had earned in my rookie season. I talked to Bennie for an hour and offered him the opportunity to grow in a Celtic uniform. He asked if I could arrange for him to play in Italy. Why? "I want to play," was all he would say.

That taught me another lesson among the many lessons I have learned. Despite all the Celtics stood for, there was someone "on the team" who did not think that playing for them was the end of the world. They had won eleven championships in thirteen years under Auerbach and Russell and one with Heinsohn coaching, but that meant absolutely nothing to Bennie Clyde. He had his own sense of values and was entitled to be right or wrong on his own as long as he was willing to pay the price.

We went on to lose the championship without Bennie, and I went home a little too early for another summer with Diane, the kids, and my folks. It had been an interesting season in many ways, though I was not sure I had convinced everyone or anyone I really was the coach of the Celtics or that I didn't snarl at my family all the time.

The Heinsohns and the in-laws have been going to the New Jersey shore for many years to relax and forget. Paul, my oldest son, was deeply into basketball, so one night I took him and a friend to the schoolyard, where we played three-on-three against some good, young players with outstanding college potential.

After the workout, we drove to a place for hamburgers and

soda. I still have a "Celtic 15" license plate, and that attracted some-one to the car. "Aren't you Tommy Heinsohn?" he asked. I nodded and expected him to seek an autograph or engage in a discussion about the Celtics' failure to win the title or the complexities of Bill Russell or whether Red Auerbach still coaches the team.

I wasn't even close. "I watch you on television all the time," said the stranger. "Why are you such a grouch? Don't you ever smile, Tommy?"

There was nothing I could say.